Summary

Chapter 18: Challenges in Implementing Collective Artificial Intelligence

18.1 Technical Challenges in CAI Implementation

18.2 Ethical Challenges in CAI Implementation

18.3 Social Challenges in CAI Implementation

Brief introduction from the author

Dear Readers,

Welcome to this book on collective artificial intelligence, a fascinating and highly relevant topic in today's world. In this work, we will explore the concepts, applications, and challenges of collective artificial intelligence, a form of intelligence that emerges from the interaction and collaboration of multiple intelligent agents, whether human, machine, or both.

Artificial intelligence is a scientific and technological discipline that seeks to create systems capable of performing tasks that normally require human intelligence, such as reasoning, learning, perception, communication, creativity, or problem solving. It is based on the study of natural intelligence, that is, the way living beings process information and adapt to their environment.

Collective intelligence, on the other hand, is the ability of a group of individuals or entities to act in a coordinated and effective way to achieve a common goal. This ability leverages the diversity, complementarity, and synergy of their knowledge, skills, and resources. Collective intelligence can manifest itself both in natural systems (ant colonies, flocks of birds, bee swarms) and in artificial systems (social networks, multi-agent systems, distributed systems).

Collective artificial intelligence combines artificial intelligence and collective intelligence. It is the creation of systems composed of multiple intelligent agents that interact and cooperate with each other to solve complex problems that exceed the individual capabilities of each agent. Collective artificial intelligence can take various forms, such as distributed artificial intelligence, hybrid artificial intelligence, participatory artificial intelligence, or augmented artificial intelligence.

In this book, we will learn about the principles, techniques, and tools that allow us to design, implement, and evaluate collective artificial intelligence systems. We will also analyze the benefits, risks, and ethical, social, and legal implications of their use. We hope that this work will be of interest to you and that it will help you better understand this fascinating field of science and technology.

Chapter 1: Introduction to Artificial Intelligence

Understanding Artificial Intelligence

Artificial intelligence (AI) is a multifaceted field of science that encompasses computer science, cognitive psychology, neuroscience, and many other disciplines. It aims to build machines capable of mimicking human intelligence by processing information and making decisions autonomously. The core objective of AI is to enable machines to perform complex tasks that would typically require human cognition—ranging from simple pattern recognition to intricate problem-solving and decision-making.

The journey into understanding AI begins with the fundamental concept of algorithms—a set of rules or instructions designed to solve problems or perform tasks. These algorithms are the building blocks of AI systems, enabling them to learn from data. Machine learning, a subset of AI, involves training these algorithms on vast amounts of data so they can improve their performance over time without being explicitly programmed for each task.

Deep learning takes this a step further by using neural networks—systems inspired by the human brain's architecture—to recognize patterns and make predictions. These networks consist of layers of interconnected nodes that process input data and generate output through activation functions. This structure allows deep learning models to handle unstructured data like images, sound, and text more effectively than traditional machine learning models.

Natural Language Processing (NLP) is another critical area within AI that focuses on the interaction between computers and humans through language. It enables machines to understand, interpret, and generate human language in a way that is both meaningful and useful. NLP applications range from chatbots providing customer service to sophisticated systems capable of translating languages or generating news articles.

AI's potential extends beyond individual tasks; it also includes autonomous systems such as self-driving cars which integrate perception, decision-making, navigation, and control to operate without human intervention. These systems rely on sensor fusion—a technique combining data from various sensors—to create accurate representations of their environment.

The Evolution of Artificial Intelligence

The evolution of artificial intelligence has been marked by several waves, each characterized by breakthroughs in technology and theory that have expanded our understanding and capabilities within the field.

In its early days during the mid-20th century, AI research was primarily theoretical with scientists exploring foundational concepts like Turing's computational theory and von Neumann's architecture for digital computers. The first wave focused on rule-based systems where knowledge was encoded into machines using if-then rules. This period saw the creation of expert systems which could mimic the decision-making abilities of a human expert in specific domains such as medical diagnosis or geological exploration.

However, these early AI systems were limited by their inability to learn or adapt beyond their initial programming. The second wave brought about machine learning where instead of being programmed explicitly for each task; machines could learn from examples. This shift was propelled forward by improvements in computational power and the availability of large datasets which allowed for more complex models that could identify patterns within data.

The advent of big data analytics has fueled this growth further leading us into what some call the third wave—an era defined by deep learning neural networks capable not only pattern recognition but also generation new content like realistic images or coherent pieces text speech synthesis another significant advancement allowing computers communicate naturally convincingly with humans.

Applications such as recommendation engines used online retailers streaming services are testament how far we've come since those early days when AI struggled basic tasks. Today these sophisticated algorithms analyze user behavior and preferences, suggest products, movies and shows likely enjoy enhancing overall experience consumers across globe.

Applications and Challenges in AI

Artificial intelligence applications permeate almost every aspect of our lives—from healthcare, finance, and entertainment to even governance—providing solutions previously thought impossible due to the sheer complexity and scale involved in managing and analyzing vast quantities of information in real time. In the healthcare sector, for example, predictive analytics powered by AI help doctors identify diseases at earlier stages, improving patient outcomes and reducing the costs associated with treatment. Similarly, the financial industry uses AI to detect fraudulent activities and secure transactions, while personalized marketing campaigns based on consumer insights are becoming the norm in the retail world, all thanks to the advancements made possible through the application of intelligent technologies.

However, despite numerous successes, there remain significant challenges facing the widespread adoption and implementation of AI. Effective and ethical use remains at the forefront of concerns, given the potential biases inherent in certain datasets used to train models. There's a risk of perpetuating existing inequalities in society. Moreover, security and privacy issues arise when dealing with sensitive personal data, especially in the context of surveillance and state-sponsored monitoring activities. Furthermore, explainability and transparency around AI decision-making processes are crucial for ensuring trust and accountability, especially in cases where wrong decisions can carry serious consequences and legal ramifications. Lastly, the economic impact and job displacement caused by automation continue to spark debate regarding the future of work and how best to prepare the workforce for the inevitable changes in the coming years.

Despite these hurdles, optimism prevails. Many believe that thoughtful regulation and collaboration among stakeholders can lead to positive outcomes for both individuals and societies. Indeed, the journey towards fully realizing AI's promise is fraught with obstacles, yet the progress made thus far suggests a bright horizon lies ahead for those willing to navigate the complexities inherent in developing and deploying responsible and impactful artificial intelligence solutions worldwide.

For those interested in delving deeper into the world of Artificial Intelligence, here are some suggested readings and references:

- 1. "Artificial Intelligence: A Modern Approach" by Stuart Russell and Peter Norvig

  This comprehensive textbook offers an in-depth overview of AI theories, techniques, and algorithms.

- 2. "Deep Learning" by Ian Goodfellow, Yoshua Bengio, and Aaron Courville

  A key resource for understanding deep learning concepts and methodologies.

- 3. "Life 3.0: Being Human in the Age of Artificial Intelligence" by Max Tegmark

  This book explores the future of AI and its impact on the fabric of human existence.

- 4. "The Master Algorithm: How the Quest for the Ultimate Learning Machine Will Remake Our World" by Pedro Domingos

  Domingos discusses machine learning and its potential to revolutionize various industries.

- 5. "Superintelligence: Paths, Dangers, Strategies" by Nick Bostrom

  An examination of the future prospects for superintelligent AI systems and how we might control their development.

- 6. Online courses from platforms like Coursera or edX offer classes from institutions such as Stanford University or MIT on AI-related topics that cater to various levels of expertise.

- 7. Research papers from journals like "Journal of Artificial Intelligence Research" (JAIR) or conferences such as NeurIPS and ICML provide cutting-edge insights into current AI advancements.

- 8. Websites like arXiv.org where preprints of research papers are shared can be a valuable resource for those who want to stay up-to-date with the latest developments in AI research.

Remember that while these resources will provide a wealth of knowledge on artificial intelligence, staying informed about ethical considerations, policy implications, and societal impacts is equally important for a well-rounded understanding of AI's role in our world.

Chapter 2: The Science Behind Artificial Intelligence

The Scientific and Technological Realm of AI

Artificial intelligence (AI) stands as a frontier in both scientific inquiry and technological innovation, where the pursuit of understanding and replicating human intelligence intersects with the development of machines capable of mimicking cognitive functions. This inherently interdisciplinary discipline draws from diverse fields such as computer science, mathematics, psychology, neuroscience, linguistics, philosophy, and even biology. At its core, AI seeks to model human intelligence by creating algorithms that can learn from data, recognize patterns, make decisions, and solve problems.

One of the foundational pillars of AI is machine learning (ML), which empowers systems to autonomously improve their performance on tasks over time without requiring explicit programming for every possible scenario. Deep learning (DL), a subset of ML inspired by the structure and function of the brain's neural networks, has played a pivotal role in advancing AI capabilities. DL utilizes multiple layers of processing to progressively extract higher-level features from raw input data.

Robotics, another critical area within AI, integrates AI with robots, enabling them to interact with the physical world through sensors and actuators. While widely utilized in manufacturing for tasks like assembly and inspection, robots are increasingly finding their way into healthcare as surgical assistants or rehabilitation aids.

Natural language processing (NLP) allows machines to understand and respond to textual or voice data in a way that feels natural to humans. This technology powers virtual assistants like Siri or Alexa and enables real-time translation services.

Computer vision equips machines with the ability to interpret visual information from their surroundings. Applications range from facial recognition software to autonomous vehicles navigating complex environments.

Expert systems, programs that mimic the decision-making abilities of human experts, and evolutionary computation, which draws inspiration from biological evolution to solve optimization and search problems, also fall under the broad umbrella of AI.

The integration of these technologies leads to the development of advanced systems capable not only of performing specific tasks but also of adapting to new situations – a characteristic known as general artificial intelligence (AGI). While AGI remains largely theoretical at this stage, its pursuit continues to drive much research within the field.

AI Systems in Action

AI systems have permeated various sectors, taking on tasks ranging from mundane to highly complex. Consumers encounter AI in their daily lives when using recommendation engines on streaming services like

Netflix or shopping platforms like Amazon. These systems analyze user behavior data to suggest products or content tailored to individual preferences.

In the financial sector, algorithms conduct high-frequency trading by analyzing market data at speeds beyond human capability. Fraud detection systems scan transactions for patterns indicative of fraudulent activity, providing security measures that dynamically adapt as scammers evolve their tactics.

Healthcare has witnessed significant advancements thanks to AI-driven diagnostic tools that can identify diseases like cancer more accurately than ever before through image recognition technologies applied to medical scans. Personalized medicine is another growing application where AI helps tailor treatments based on an individual's genetic makeup.

Smart cities leverage AI for traffic management, optimizing signal timings based on real-time flow conditions to reduce congestion and pollution levels. Waste management systems utilize sensors combined with predictive analytics to ensure efficient collection routes, saving time and resources while maintaining clean urban spaces.

In education, adaptive learning platforms utilize student performance data to personalize educational experiences, meeting learners' unique needs and pace, and fostering better engagement and outcomes throughout the learning process.

Studying Natural Intelligence to Advance AI

Understanding natural intelligence provides invaluable insights into the development of sophisticated artificial systems. By studying how humans think, learn, and perceive, researchers gain valuable clues for designing more effective algorithms and architectures that underpin intelligent behavior in machines.

The Crucial Role of Cognitive Science and Neuroscience in AI Development

Cognitive science plays a vital role in the advancement of AI. It examines various mental processes including memory, problem-solving, attention, language acquisition, and more, potentially offering models applicable to computational contexts. For example, insights into how children acquire language have informed the development of natural language processing (NLP) techniques, while understanding visual perception has guided improvements in computer vision algorithms.

Neuroscience offers another potent source of knowledge by exploring the brain's structure and function down to the cellular level. This reveals the mechanisms behind thought, emotion, and even consciousness itself. Findings regarding neuroplasticity—the brain's ability to adapt and change in response to experience—have significant implications for the design of flexible and adaptable neural network-based AI systems. These systems, like humans, could evolve over time through exposure to new information and experiences.

Furthermore, ethology, the study of animal behavior, contributes to our understanding of collective behaviors and social structures observed in nature. These insights inform the development of swarm robotics and multi-agent system simulations that mimic the coordination seen in ant colonies, bird flocks, and bee swarms. By effectively leveraging group dynamics rather than solely relying on individual agent capabilities, such systems broaden the scope and potential applications of collective artificial intelligence far beyond what a single entity could achieve on its own.

For those interested in delving deeper into the field of AI, here are some suggested readings and references:

1."Artificial Intelligence: A Modern Approach" by Stuart Russell and Peter Norvig. This textbook offers a comprehensive overview of AI theories, techniques, and the state of the art.

2."Deep Learning" by Ian Goodfellow, Yoshua Bengio, and Aaron Courville. This book provides an in-depth look at deep learning architectures and their applications.

3."Life 3.0: Being Human in the Age of Artificial Intelligence" by Max Tegmark. Tegmark explores the future of AI and its impact on society.

4."The Master Algorithm: How the Quest for the Ultimate Learning Machine Will Remake Our World" by Pedro Domingos. Domingos discusses machine learning and its potential to transform various industries.

5."Superintelligence: Paths, Dangers, Strategies" by Nick Bostrom. Bostrom examines the future prospects of artificial intelligence and its ethical implications.

These resources offer a mix of technical knowledge, philosophical insights, and discussions about AI's broader societal effects, suitable for readers ranging from students to professionals in the field.

Chapter 3: Collective Intelligence: An Overview

Defining Collective Intelligence

For decades, collective intelligence has captivated philosophers, scientists, and technologists. At its core, it denotes the enhanced problem-solving, innovation, and creation capacity achieved when individuals or entities collaborate. This phenomenon transcends the abilities of any individual member and emerges from the interactions and collaborations within the collective.

The roots of collective intelligence lie in early human societies, where survival depended on effective collaboration. Technology has expanded this concept in modern times, enabling collaboration across vast distances and among diverse entities, including machines. The internet's advent has particularly amplified our collective intelligence capacity by facilitating unprecedented instant communication and information sharing.

Defining collective intelligence necessitates distinguishing mere aggregation of individual efforts from a truly synergistic process. The latter involves complex interactions where participants not only contribute but also adapt in response to others' contributions. This dynamic process often leads to novel insights or solutions unattainable individually.

Wikipedia serves as an illustrative example. It harnesses the knowledge of thousands of diverse contributors worldwide, bringing unique expertise and perspectives. The platform's structure facilitates coordination and content refinement through continuous editing and discussion, resulting in a rich knowledge repository no single contributor could create alone.

Another example is open-source software development, where projects like Linux or Apache thrive on collective intelligence. Developers from around the globe contribute code, identify bugs, enhance features, and support users. This collaborative nature ensures these projects evolve much faster than traditional closed development models.

Collective intelligence also manifests in natural systems like ant colonies or bee swarms, where simple creatures follow basic rules but collectively exhibit sophisticated behaviors. Finding the shortest path to food sources or selecting optimal nesting sites—tasks seemingly beyond their individual cognitive capabilities—exemplify this.

As we delve deeper into defining collective intelligence, we must consider its applicability not just in cooperative endeavors but also in competitive environments like financial markets, where traders collectively determine asset prices based on varying strategies and information interpretations.

Understanding collective intelligence requires examining information flow within groups, decision-making processes, participation motivations, and conflict resolution, all factors influencing the effectiveness of a collective system.

The Power of Group Coordination and Efficiency

Realizing the power inherent in collective intelligence hinges on group coordination. When individuals align their efforts towards a common goal efficiently, they can achieve outcomes far exceeding those possible through isolated action.

Several factors contribute to efficient coordination: clear communication channels, shared objectives, trust among members, appropriate incentive structures, effective leadership or governance mechanisms, and robust interaction platforms.

Disaster response scenarios, where multiple agencies must collaborate swiftly amidst chaos, exemplify this. Effective coordination can be the difference between life and death as resources are deployed urgently without duplication of effort or critical gaps in response.

In business contexts, companies like Toyota demonstrate how empowering workers at all levels to contribute ideas for process improvement can lead to significant efficiency gains through "kaizen," or continuous improvement. This principle recognizes the value each individual brings to a collaborative effort.

Technology plays an increasingly vital role in facilitating group coordination by providing tools for project management (Trello), real-time communication (Slack), decision-making support (Loomio), and more.

These tools aim to streamline collaboration regardless of physical distance.

Furthermore, research into swarm robotics draws inspiration from nature's examples of efficient group coordination. Systems are created where robots communicate with simple signals yet collectively perform complex tasks, such as search-and-rescue operations or environmental monitoring, with high efficiency due to their coordinated behavior patterns.

Challenges of Efficient Group Coordination

Achieving efficient group coordination is not without its challenges. Overcoming barriers related to cultural differences, managing conflicts, ensuring equitable participation, dealing with free riders, adapting quickly to changing situations, and maintaining motivation over time are all areas requiring careful consideration when designing systems for collaborative use, whether involving humans, machines, or both.

Diversity, Complementarity, and Synergy: Pillars of Collective Intelligence

The concepts of diversity, complementarity, and synergy are the central pillars upon which collective intelligence stands. They represent different aspects that, when combined effectively, result in a whole greater than the sum of its parts.

- Diversity refers to the variety of backgrounds, skills, and perspectives brought together within a group. It's a well-documented phenomenon that diverse teams tend to produce more innovative solutions because they draw on a wider range of experiences and viewpoints. This diversity of thought processes helps avoid the pitfalls of groupthink and encourages creative problem-solving. For example, multinational corporations leverage employee diversity to foster innovation on a global scale by tapping into local market insights and cultural nuances that drive product development and marketing strategies.

- Complementarity deals with the way different elements within a group fit together harmoniously. Each member contributes a unique set of skills, knowledge, and resources, filling the gaps left by others, thereby creating a comprehensive toolkit to tackle challenges. A classic case of complementarity can be seen in jazz ensembles, where musicians play different instruments and roles yet come together to create a cohesive piece of music. Each musician's contribution complements the others, resulting in a sound richer and more complex than any instrument could produce alone.

- Synergy occurs when the interaction between these diverse and complementary elements leads to outcomes impossible to achieve independently. This term is often used to describe the "magic" that happens when team members click and work in unison towards a shared vision. Anecdotal evidence abounds: successful sports teams and startups attribute part of their success to synergistic dynamics. But there is also a scientific basis for understanding synergy. For instance, studies show that brainstorming sessions structured to encourage positive reinforcement and constructive criticism yield better ideas compared to sessions dominated by competition and criticism.

These three components—diversity, complementarity, and synergy—are not just beneficial; they are necessary ingredients for a successful collective endeavor. Understanding and leveraging them means recognizing and valuing differences, fostering an environment of mutual respect, and building frameworks that allow for the seamless integration of efforts. Ultimately, the aim is to maximize the potential of every participant while steering clear of the pitfalls of homogeneity, discord, and inefficiency.

Real-world Examples and Significance

Real-world applications abound—from interdisciplinary research tackling climate change to tech companies assembling cross-functional teams to develop cutting-edge products. These examples underscore the importance of embracing diversity, seeking out complementary skill sets, and nurturing synergistic relationships to unlock the full potential of collective intelligence. Whether addressing societal challenges, driving innovation in the workplace, or simply collaborating effectively, cultivating these three elements remains key to unlocking the boundless possibilities collaboration offers.

For further reading on collective intelligence and its implications, consider the following references:

- 1."The Wisdom of Crowds" by James Surowiecki – This book explores how large groups of people can be smarter than an elite few, no matter how brilliant—better at solving problems, fostering innovation, coming to wise decisions, even predicting the future.

- 2."Reinventing Organizations" by Frederic Laloux – Laloux examines historical management styles and emerging organizational structures that leverage collective intelligence in innovative ways.

- 3."Superminds: The Surprising Power of People and Computers Thinking Together" by Thomas W. Malone – Malone discusses how computers can help create more intelligent organizations that are competitive in today's economic landscape.

- 4."Collective Intelligence: Creating a Prosperous World at Peace" edited by Mark Tovey – A collection of essays from various authors discussing the potential for collective intelligence to solve complex global issues.

- 5."Smart Swarms: The New Decision Science Inspired by Nature's Most Clever Creatures" by Peter Miller – This book looks at how animals work together and what humans can learn from them about collective behavior.

- 6.Research articles from journals such as the Journal of Collective Intelligence, which provide academic insights into the mechanisms and applications of collective intelligence across different fields.

These resources offer a blend of theoretical perspectives, practical insights, and case studies that illustrate the power and challenges of harnessing collective intelligence in various contexts.

Chapter 4: Manifestations of Collective Intelligence

Collective Intelligence in Natural Systems: A Testament to Evolution and Adaptation

The concept of collective intelligence in natural systems is a testament to the remarkable capabilities of evolution and adaptation. In these systems, individual organisms work together, often without centralized control, to achieve complex tasks beyond the reach of single entities. This form of intelligence is not only fascinating but also serves as an inspiration for developing advanced artificial systems.

Examples from the Insect World:

- Ants: They exhibit sophisticated colony behaviors through simple interactions. Pheromones communicate paths to food or danger, allowing them to adapt quickly and allocate resources efficiently.

- Bees: Collective decision-making shines during hive selection. Scout bees evaluate potential sites and report back through a "dance language," with the swarm reaching consensus through a complex mechanism for optimal survival.

Beyond Insects:

- Migratory birds: Starlings perform mesmerizing "murmurations" thought to be defensive maneuvers, emerging from simple rules followed by each bird.

- Fish schools: These synchronize movements to confuse predators and increase efficiency during migration, enhancing foraging and reproduction.

These phenomena highlight how collective behavior can lead to intelligent outcomes without individual understanding of the overall pattern or goal. They offer valuable insights for designing distributed problem-solving strategies in robotics, computer science, and environmental management.

Collective Intelligence in Artificial Systems:

Artificial systems mimic the collaborative essence of natural collectives with unique technological twists. Networks of computers or robots work together towards common goals, from solving computational problems to performing physical tasks.

Key Areas:

- Multi-agent systems (MAS): Autonomous agents with specific skills collaborate or compete within an environment to achieve shared goals, like robotic soccer teams where each robot adapts strategies based on teammates and opponents.

- Distributed computing: Tasks are divided among multiple networked computers, collectively processing large datasets much faster than a single machine. Projects like SETI@home analyze radio signals for extraterrestrial life using internet-connected computers worldwide.

- Social networking platforms: Human input combines with algorithmic processing to curate content, personalize experiences, and facilitate connections, leading to emergent behaviors like viral trends or crowd-sourced problem-solving.

- Machine learning advancements: Deep learning has led to neural network architectures capable of collaborating on complex tasks like image recognition, language translation, or playing strategic games like Go at superhuman levels, demonstrating how machines can develop "swarm" intelligence akin to biological counterparts.

Comparing Natural and Artificial Systems:

Both operate under similar principles: local interactions leading to global patterns. However, key differences exist due to design versus evolution constraints:

- Natural systems: Evolved over millions of years, resulting in highly efficient resource utilization and resilience against failure due to biological redundancy.

- Artificial systems: Designed by humans, tend to be more specialized and less robust, lacking the evolutionary pressures shaping their natural counterparts. However, they benefit from the ability to rapidly iterate and improve upon designs thanks to our understanding of engineering and computation.

Additional Key Differences:

- Intentionality: In natural systems (ant colonies, bee swarms), no single entity has an overarching plan, yet they achieve remarkable feats. In contrast, MAS and distributed computing networks are generally programmed with specific intentions, whether optimizing traffic flow or coordinating drones for agricultural monitoring.

- Communication: Nature's signaling mechanisms use chemical, visual, and auditory cues, while artificial entities utilize digital protocols and data streams. This highlights the fundamental difference between organic and synthetic forms of communication, impacting speed, reliability, and scalability.

- Adaptability and Flexibility: Organisms within ecosystems must continuously adapt to survive changing conditions. Many current AI models struggle to generalize beyond training data, highlighting the gap between adaptive capacities of living beings and those created in silicon. However, ongoing research in reinforcement learning and evolutionary algorithms aims to bridge this divide, enabling more dynamic and responsive artificial collectives in the future.

Conclusion:

Examining collective intelligence across both natural and artificial realms provides us with a profound appreciation for the interconnectedness of all things. Whether observing a flock of birds executing a perfect turn or marveling at the efficiency of a server farm processing petabytes of data, it is clear that collaboration is key to unlocking higher levels of functionality and sophistication across the spectrum of existence.

Chapter 5: Unveiling Collective Artificial Intelligence

Harnessing the Synergy of AI and Collective Intelligence

The fusion of artificial intelligence (AI) with collective intelligence (CI) represents a transformative approach that leverages the strengths of both human and machine cognition. This synergy aims to create systems that are more adaptive, resilient, and capable than either AI or human efforts alone. By integrating the nuanced understanding and creativity of humans with the speed, accuracy, and tireless processing power of AI, we can tackle challenges that were previously insurmountable.

A Powerful Blend in Action:

One compelling example lies in citizen science projects like Galaxy Zoo, where volunteers classify galaxies by type. Here, collective human intelligence contributes to massive data analysis tasks that would be overwhelming for individual researchers or automated systems. When combined with machine learning algorithms that learn from the classifications to improve their own performance, we see a powerful blend of CI and AI working in tandem.

This combination is also revolutionizing industries such as healthcare. Platforms leveraging CI engage numerous medical professionals to collectively diagnose complex cases while AI tools analyze vast datasets to identify patterns and suggest treatments. This collaborative effort not only improves diagnostic accuracy but also accelerates the discovery of novel therapeutic strategies.

Designing Effective Amalgamation:

Creating an effective amalgamation of AI and CI requires careful consideration of how humans and machines interact. It's crucial to design interfaces that facilitate seamless communication between agents and leverage their respective strengths. For instance, in financial markets, AI can process market data at incredible speeds while human traders provide strategic oversight based on their experience and intuition about market sentiment.

New Horizons for Problem-Solving:

In summary, combining AI with CI opens up new horizons for problem-solving across various domains. It allows us to tackle large-scale issues by distributing tasks among diverse agents while maintaining a cohesive strategy towards achieving common goals.

Multi-Agent Intelligent Systems: Orchestrating Collaboration

Multi-agent intelligent systems (MAIS) represent a paradigm shift in conceptualizing problem-solving within AI frameworks. These systems consist of multiple autonomous agents that interact within an environment to achieve both individual objectives and a shared purpose. The complexity lies not just in designing each agent but also in orchestrating their interactions to produce emergent behaviors beneficial for solving intricate problems.

Smart Grid Example:

A quintessential example is found within smart grid technology where numerous agents representing different components—such as consumers, energy storage systems, renewable energy sources—work together to optimize energy distribution and consumption. Each agent operates autonomously yet must communicate effectively with others to balance supply and demand dynamically.

Building Effective MAIS:

Constructing such MAIS effectively requires sophisticated algorithms that govern agent behavior, including negotiation protocols, decision-making models, and learning mechanisms that enable adaptation over time. Furthermore, these systems must be robust against failures, ensuring that if one agent goes offline, others can compensate accordingly—a concept known as fault tolerance.

Another critical aspect is scalability. As more agents join the system, it should continue functioning efficiently without significant degradation in performance or increase in complexity for each additional agent. This scalability is vital for applications like traffic management where hundreds or even thousands of agents—from traffic lights to vehicle control systems—must work harmoniously.

Ultimately, creating MAIS demands interdisciplinary expertise drawing from computer science, psychology, economics, game theory, and other fields, all contributing insights into how intelligent entities should interact within complex environments.

Collective Artificial Intelligence: Tackling Daunting Problems

Collective Artificial Intelligence (CAI) has emerged as a potent tool for tackling some of the most daunting problems facing humanity today, ranging from climate change mitigation to managing global pandemics. By leveraging the distributed nature of CAI, we can integrate diverse perspectives, datasets, and computational techniques, leading to solutions far beyond what any single agent could achieve alone.

Illustrative Case: Urban Planning:

Take urban planning as an illustrative case. CAI enables us to simulate entire cities populated by intelligent agents representing individuals, businesses, vehicles, etc., each with unique behaviors but interacting within a shared virtual space. Planners can experiment with different policies, observing how changes affect traffic patterns, pollution levels, and economic activity, providing invaluable insights before implementing real-world interventions.

Addressing Complexity and Uncertainty:

Furthermore, CAI excels at addressing problems characterized by high uncertainty or complexity, such as disaster response operations where multiple organizations must coordinate relief efforts under rapidly changing conditions. Here, CAI facilitates real-time information sharing, decision support, and predictive modeling, ensuring resources are deployed where they're needed most efficiently.

Challenges and the Future:

Yet, realizing this potential isn't without challenges. It necessitates advanced infrastructure capable of supporting extensive data exchange, high-performance computing, alongside robust security measures protecting against malicious actors who might seek to disrupt these complex networks.

In conclusion, collective artificial intelligence (CAI) represents an evolutionary leap forward, empowering us to collectively confront issues whose scale and intricacy would otherwise overwhelm traditional approaches. Whether it involves simulating intricate ecosystems, optimizing sprawling industrial processes, or fostering collaboration across global teams, CAI's impact continues to grow, shaping future innovation across countless domains.

Chapter 6: Forms of Collective Artificial intelligence

Distributed Artificial Intelligence: Collaboration for Complex Problem-Solving

Distributed Artificial Intelligence (DAI) represents a fascinating subfield of AI concerned with developing decentralized systems composed of multiple interacting intelligent agents. These agents, ranging from software to hardware, collaborate to tackle problems too complex for individual entities. The fundamental principles of DAI revolve around coordination, cooperation, and negotiation among agents to achieve a shared goal.

Parallelizing Solutions with Teamwork:

One of DAI's key strengths lies in its ability to parallelize problem-solving. By distributing tasks across various agents, the system can tackle different aspects of a problem simultaneously, leading to faster and more efficient solutions. This approach shines in domains like logistics and supply chain management, where multiple entities must coordinate actions. For instance, modern warehouses leverage collaborative autonomous robots to sort and transport goods, optimizing the overall workflow.

Sensor Networks: Seeing the Bigger Picture:

Another significant application area for DAI is in distributed sensor networks. Here, numerous sensors independently collect data but work together to analyze environmental conditions or monitor security threats.

Disaster response scenarios exemplify this effectively, where sensor networks share information across nodes, aiding in damage assessment and identification of safe evacuation routes.

Smart Grids: Powering the Future Collectively:

DAI also plays a crucial role in smart grids for electricity distribution. In this context, various components like substations, transformers, and consumer homes equipped with smart meters form an intelligent network that manages energy flow efficiently. Through real-time communication and adaptive decision-making among these components, smart grids dynamically balance supply and demand while seamlessly integrating renewable energy sources.

Challenges and the Road Ahead:

While DAI offers immense potential, challenges remain. Ensuring robust communication protocols among agents is crucial to prevent misunderstandings and conflicts that could lead to suboptimal outcomes. Additionally, designing these systems requires careful consideration of how individual agent goals align with the collective objective without compromising autonomy.

As we move towards an increasingly connected world with IoT devices permeating every aspect of our lives, from home automation to urban planning, DAI will become even more integral. It will not only enhance operational efficiency but also enable unprecedented forms of collaboration between machines and humans alike.

Hybrid Participatory Artificial Intelligence: Humans and Machines, United

Hybrid Participatory Artificial Intelligence (HPAI) represents an innovative convergence where human intelligence and artificial intelligence systems collaborate towards common objectives. This hybrid model leverages both human creativity and machine efficiency to address complex issues that neither could effectively solve alone.

Citizen Science: Crowdsourcing the Cosmos:

In HPAI systems, humans contribute through decision-making guidance, creative insights, or data collection efforts. Citizen science projects like Galaxy Zoo showcase this effectively. Volunteers classify galaxies by shape, a task challenging for AI due to subtle nuances. Their efforts are complemented by machine learning algorithms that learn from these classifications to automate parts of the process.

Crowdsourcing Innovation:

Crowdsourcing platforms further exemplify HPAI, where individuals offer solutions or ideas that are then sifted through by AI-driven analysis tools to identify the most promising ones quickly. This synergy significantly accelerates innovation cycles compared with traditional R&D methods.

Challenges and Ethical Considerations:

Implementing HPAI comes with its own set of challenges. Ensuring meaningful human participation without overwhelming contributors with complexity is crucial. Additionally, transparency regarding how AI utilizes human input within these systems is paramount.

Furthermore, ethical considerations around data privacy become paramount when personal information is involved, requiring stringent measures for protection against misuse or unauthorized access.

The Future of Healthcare:

Looking ahead, we might see HPAI extensively employed in healthcare diagnostics. Patient input combined with advanced medical imaging analyzed by AI could lead to personalized treatment plans offering better outcomes than current standards allow.

Augmented Artificial Intelligence: Empowering Human Potential

Augmented Artificial Intelligence (AAI) refers to systems designed not just for automating tasks but for enhancing human cognitive abilities through seamless integration with AI technologies. AAI aims to amplify human potential rather than replace it, providing tools that assist us in making better decisions based on augmented data analysis capabilities provided by artificial intelligence.

Business Intelligence: Insights at Your Fingertips:

Business intelligence platforms utilizing AAI exemplify this well. Executives use sophisticated dashboards powered by underlying machine learning models that analyze vast amounts of market data, providing actionable insights enabling informed strategic decisions beyond what's possible manually due to sheer volume and complexity.

Art Meets Technology:

AAI's impact extends to creative industries as well. Music composition software incorporating AI elements allows musicians to explore new soundscapes, guided yet not limited by algorithmic suggestions based on learned preferences and styles. This interplay fosters innovation while retaining artistic control over the final output.

Challenges and the Balancing Act:

Deploying AAI isn't without its challenges. One major concern revolves around user trust, especially when system recommendations carry significant weight, such as in financial investment advice or medical diagnoses. Building reliable and transparent interfaces that clearly explain the reasoning behind suggestions becomes critical in these situations.

Additionally, there's a risk associated with over-reliance on technology. If not balanced properly, excessive dependence on AAI could diminish our own skills, a phenomenon known as "automation complacency." This highlights the importance of striking a balance between leveraging technology's power and maintaining our own critical thinking and decision-making abilities.

Revolutionizing Education:

Despite these challenges, the potential benefits of AAI are immense. The education sector stands to gain significantly from personalized learning experiences tailored to individual student needs. This could revolutionize the way knowledge is imparted and assessed, leading to greater engagement, mastery, and overall understanding of subjects.

Collective Intelligence: Shaping the Future:

In conclusion, each form of collective artificial intelligence presents unique opportunities and challenges that will shape future interactions between humans and machines. As these technologies continue to evolve, so too will the ways we leverage their strengths to create smarter, more responsive systems capable of tackling both today's pressing issues and the unforeseen challenges of tomorrow.

For further reading and references on these topics, you might consider the following sources:

- 1.Distributed Artificial Intelligence:

  Weiss, G. (Ed.). (2013). Multiagent Systems (2nd ed.). MIT Press. This book provides a comprehensive introduction to the theory and practice of multiagent systems, including distributed AI.

  Wooldridge, M., & Jennings, N. R. (1995). Intelligent agents: Theory and practice. The Knowledge Engineering Review, 10(2), 115-

152.This paper offers foundational concepts in agent-based and multi-agent systems.

- 2.Hybrid Participatory Artificial Intelligence:

O'Reilly, T., & Tushman, M. L. (2013). Organizational Ambidexterity: Past, Present, and Future. Academy of Management Perspectives, 27(4), 324-

338.This article discusses organizational strategies that balance exploration and exploitation, relevant to HPAI.

Hecker, D., & Haklay, M. (Eds.). (2018). Citizen Science: Innovation in Open Science, Society and Policy. UCL Press. This book explores citizen science as a form of participatory research.

- 3.Augmented Artificial Intelligence:

Davenport, T.H., & Kirby J. (2016). Only Humans Need Apply: Winners and Losers in the Age of Smart Machines. Harper Business. The book discusses how AI can augment human jobs rather than replace them.

Bostrom, N., & Yudkowsky E.(2014). The Ethics of Artificial Intelligence.The Cambridge Handbook of Artificial Intelligence.Cambridge University Press.This chapter addresses ethical considerations related to AI.

Remember that while these sources provide a solid foundation for understanding these areas of AI research and application, staying current with the latest developments requires accessing recent journal articles and conference proceedings due to the fast-paced nature of technology advancements in AI.

Please note that some sources may not be freely available without institutional access or purchase; however abstracts or summaries can often provide useful insights into the content discussed within each work.

Chapter 7: Principles of Designing CAI systems

The Cornerstones of Collective Artificial Intelligence: Core Principles and Design Techniques

Understanding the design principles of collective artificial intelligence (CAI) systems is crucial for comprehending how these intricate entities operate and interact. At its heart, CAI harnesses the combined power of multiple intelligent agents to tackle goals beyond the reach of individual agents. To achieve this effectively, designers must consider a range of principles governing system architecture, agent behavior, communication protocols, and learning mechanisms.

Decentralization: Strength in Distribution

Unlike traditional AI systems built around a central processing unit or algorithm, CAI systems distribute tasks across a network of agents. This not only enhances scalability but also bolsters robustness and resilience against system failures or attacks. For instance, in distributed sensor networks used for environmental monitoring, each sensor operates independently yet contributes to a collective understanding of the environment's condition.

Heterogeneity: Diversity Breeds Innovation

In CAI systems, agent diversity—whether in capabilities, knowledge bases, or problem-solving approaches—can fuel more innovative solutions and improve overall performance. Imagine diverse robots collaborating in a search-and-rescue operation: aerial drones providing aerial reconnaissance while ground units navigate debris to locate survivors.

Interoperability: Bridging the Gap Between Diverse Entities

Agents within a CAI system must effectively communicate and coordinate actions despite differences in design or function. This necessitates standardized communication protocols and interfaces for seamless interaction among diverse components.

Learning and Adaptation: Continuous Improvement

Effective CAI systems require agents capable of learning from experiences and adapting their strategies based on new information or environmental changes. Machine learning algorithms play a significant role here, enabling agents to improve over time without explicit reprogramming.

Ethical Considerations: Ensuring AI Acts for Good

Ethical considerations are paramount when designing CAI systems. As these systems often operate with high autonomy and can have significant societal impacts, embedding ethical decision-making processes within them is essential to ensure they act in ways that are beneficial—or at least not harmful—to humans.

Crafting Effective CAI Systems: Design Techniques

Designing effective CAI systems necessitates utilizing various techniques that address the unique challenges posed by multi-agent collaboration.

Sophisticated Agent Interaction Models:

One approach involves crafting sophisticated models for agent interaction that can predict outcomes based on different cooperation strategies. Game theory provides valuable insights here, helping designers understand how autonomous agents might behave in competitive or cooperative scenarios.

Modular Design: Breaking Down Complexity

Modular design allows individual components or agents within a CAI system to be developed separately before integration into the larger whole. This facilitates easier updates and maintenance, and allows teams to work concurrently on different aspects of the system.

Simulation: Virtual Testing Grounds

Before deploying a real-world CAI system, designers often use simulations to test different configurations and strategies in controlled virtual environments. These simulations can reveal potential coordination or performance issues that might not be apparent from theoretical models alone.

Agent-Based Modeling (ABM): Unveiling Emergent Behavior

ABM, where each agent is modeled as an independent "actor" with its own set of behaviors and interactions, is another powerful technique. ABMs help in understanding emergent behavior—the complex phenomena arising from simple interactions—characteristic of many natural and social systems.

Continuous Improvement Through Feedback Loops

Incorporating feedback loops into the design process ensures continuous improvement of CAI systems post-deployment. By analyzing data generated during operation, such as successful strategies or bottlenecks, designers can iteratively refine agent algorithms and interaction protocols.

By understanding these core principles and design techniques, we can create effective CAI systems that harness the power of collective intelligence to solve complex challenges and shape a better future.

Tools for Building Powerful Collective AI Solutions: A basic guide

The successful implementation of collective artificial intelligence (CAI) systems hinges on sophisticated tools that support development across the entire lifecycle, from initial conception to ongoing maintenance. Here's an overview of key tools that empower CAI developers:

Integrated Development Environments (IDEs):

Specifically designed for AI development, these comprehensive suites integrate coding, testing, debugging, and deployment functionalities for intelligent agents within a single environment. Many IDEs even include pre-built libraries for tasks like natural language processing and image recognition, significantly accelerating development.

Middleware Platforms:

Tailored for multi-agent systems, these platforms offer essential services like message passing interfaces for agent communication and directory services to track active agents within the network.

Machine Learning Frameworks:

For adaptive CAI systems, tools like TensorFlow and PyTorch are invaluable. They enable developers to build complex neural networks that learn from vast datasets over time through deep learning techniques.

Cloud Computing Resources:

When implementing large-scale CAI applications, cloud computing comes to the rescue. It provides on-demand access to scalable storage and computational power, eliminating the need for significant upfront investments in physical infrastructure.

Simulation Software:

Specialized simulation software empowers designers to not only test but also visualize how multiple agents will interact within virtual environments. This virtual testing ground minimizes deployment risks and ensures optimal configuration before real-world application.

Conclusion:

Understanding the principles of effective CAI design, employing the right development techniques, and leveraging appropriate tools throughout the implementation journey are all crucial for building powerful AI collaborations that can tackle today's most challenging problems across various sectors, from industry and healthcare to education and beyond. As these technologies continue to evolve, ensuring their responsible and innovative development remains paramount for the future of AI research and practice.

For further reading on the principles, techniques, and tools for designing and implementing Collective Artificial Intelligence (CAI) systems, consider exploring the following references:

- 1.Wooldridge, M. (2009). An Introduction to MultiAgent Systems. John Wiley & Sons.

  A comprehensive textbook providing an overview of multi-agent systems and their applications.

- 2.Weiss, G. (Ed.). (2013). Multiagent Systems. MIT Press.

  A collection of essays by leading researchers in the field of multi-agent systems.

- 3.Sutton, R. S., & Barto, A. G. (2018). Reinforcement Learning: An Introduction (2nd ed.). MIT Press.

  This book offers a thorough introduction to reinforcement learning, a key technique in adaptive CAI systems.

- 4.Russell, S., & Norvig, P. (2020). Artificial Intelligence: A Modern Approach (4th ed.). Pearson.

  The latest edition of this classic AI textbook includes discussions relevant to collective intelligence.

- 5.Tumer, K., & Wolpert, D. H. (Eds.). (2004). Collectives and the Design of Complex Systems. Springer.

  This edited volume explores how collectives can be leveraged to design complex systems effectively.

- 6.Panait, L., & Luke, S. (2005). Cooperative Multi-Agent Learning: The State of the Art. Autonomous Agents and Multi-Agent Systems, 11(3), 387-

  A survey paper that reviews state-of-the-art cooperative learning approaches in multi-agent systems.

These resources provide foundational knowledge as well as advanced insights into CAI system design and implementation strategies suitable for academics and practitioners alike interested in artificial intelligence research and development.

Chapter 8: Evaluating CAI systems

The evaluation of Collective Artificial Intelligence (CAI) systems stands as a critical pillar in their development and deployment. It acts as a stringent quality assurance process, guaranteeing that these intricate systems fulfill their intended goals, perform efficiently, and adhere to ethical principles. To overlook this rigorous assessment would be akin to building upon unreliable foundations, potentially jeopardizing the effectiveness, user acceptance, and overall societal impact of CAI.

The benefits gleaned from evaluating CAI systems are myriad. Firstly, it acts as a powerful tool for unearthing both the strengths and weaknesses within the system. Through meticulously testing its capabilities and performance across diverse conditions, developers can pinpoint areas requiring refinement or improvement. This continuous feedback loop fuels an iterative design process, ultimately enhancing both the functionality and user experience of the CAI system.

Furthermore, evaluation plays a pivotal role in fostering trust and credibility among users and stakeholders. A meticulously evaluated CAI system exudes an aura of reliability and safety, essential for garnering public confidence, particularly when these systems are implemented in sensitive domains such as healthcare, finance, or autonomous transportation. Imagine entrusting your health to an AI-powered diagnostic tool or relinquishing control of your vehicle to a self-driving car without the assurance of comprehensive evaluation!

Beyond the realm of functionality, evaluating CAI systems delves into their societal impact, examining how they influence human behavior, societal norms, and group decision-making processes. Such assessments become even more crucial in light of potential biases that might arise from the data or algorithms employed by CAI systems. Vigilant evaluation helps prevent discriminatory or unfair treatment of specific individuals or groups, safeguarding against the perpetuation of societal inequalities through technology.

The knowledge gleaned from evaluations also contributes significantly to the advancement of the field itself. By providing empirical evidence of what works and what doesn't, these assessments become invaluable resources for researchers striving to push the boundaries of collective intelligence and its integration with artificial intelligence. Imagine the exponential leap in progress that could be achieved if researchers had access to a comprehensive library of evaluation results, highlighting both successes and pitfalls!

Finally, in an era where governments are increasingly crafting legislation governing the use of AI technologies, demonstrating compliance through rigorous evaluation becomes paramount for legal operation. Without such proof, even the most well-intentioned CAI system could face roadblocks in its implementation, hindering its potential to contribute positively to society.

Given the inherent complexity and diverse applications of CAI systems, their evaluation necessitates a multifaceted approach. A range of methods have been developed to effectively assess different aspects of these systems:

- Simulation-based Testing: By constructing virtual environments that mimic real-world scenarios, evaluators can observe the system's responses in a controlled setting, mitigating the risks associated with real-world deployment.

- User-Centric Evaluation: This method focuses on the human-computer interaction, measuring factors like ease of use, learnability, cognitive load, and user satisfaction. Tools like surveys, interviews, task analysis, eye-tracking studies, and A/B testing provide valuable insights into the user experience.

- Performance Metrics: Quantitative data on accuracy, efficiency, robustness, scalability, and other key performance indicators provide objective measures for comparison against benchmarks or development goals.

- Ethical Evaluations: Examining aspects like transparency, fairness, privacy, accountability, and other ethical considerations through established frameworks ensures that CAI systems operate within a responsible and socially conscious framework.

- Field Trials: Deploying a prototype CAI system in its intended context with real users allows researchers to collect real-time data on its performance in actual situations, providing invaluable insights for further refinement.

Case studies offer concrete examples of how these diverse methods can be applied effectively across different sectors:

- Healthcare: Imagine a distributed AI diagnostic tool undergoing clinical trials with patients from diverse backgrounds to ensure accuracy across different demographics, while simultaneously conducting usability tests with medical staff who will regularly interact with the system.

- Finance: An automated trading platform employing collective intelligence algorithms could be tested through simulations designed for volatile market conditions, ensuring its robustness against unexpected economic events. Additionally, ethical reviews would focus on preventing manipulative practices that could harm market integrity.

- Autonomous Vehicles: Field trials play a crucial role in this domain. Imagine self-driving cars undergoing rigorous testing on closed tracks before venturing onto public roads under strict supervision. Data would be collected on safety performance in various traffic conditions, weather patterns, and pedestrian behaviors. Alongside these tests, community feedback sessions would gauge public sentiment towards the integration of such technology into daily life.

These case studies not only showcase practical applications but also highlight the challenges encountered during evaluations. Balancing thoroughness with resource constraints, managing stakeholder expectations, and dealing with unforeseen complications arising during live tests are just some of the hurdles that evaluators must overcome. However, the valuable lessons learned from these challenges provide invaluable insights for future projects within this rapidly evolving domain.

In conclusion, the evaluation of CAI systems is not merely a peripheral step in their development and deployment; it stands as a cornerstone for building trust.

Chapter 9: Benefits of Using CAI systems

The Dawn of Collective Artificial Intelligence: Shaping a Brighter Future

The arrival of collective artificial intelligence (CAI) systems signals a transformative era in technological advancement, where the confluence of human and machine intelligence unlocks unprecedented problem-solving and innovation potential. The benefits of CAI are extensive and diverse, weaving their influence into virtually every aspect of human endeavor.

One of the most significant contributions of CAI lies in its ability to elevate decision-making processes. These systems possess the remarkable capacity to analyze vast quantities of data, far exceeding human capability, uncovering patterns and insights that would otherwise remain hidden. This talent finds its application in various fields, such as healthcare. Here, CAI can analyze medical records to aid in diagnosing diseases or even recommending personalized treatment plans. In the realm of finance, these systems can monitor market trends and risks in real-time, providing investors with informed guidance on their portfolios.

Beyond their analytical prowess, CAI systems also excel at fostering creativity and innovation. By combining the intuitive leaps of human thought with the computational might of AI, these systems can help design ingenious solutions to complex problems. Imagine engineering, for instance, where CAI facilitates the creation of more efficient structures or machines by simulating countless design variations with remarkable speed.

Furthermore, CAI holds the potential to democratize expertise by making specialized knowledge more accessible. Educational platforms powered by CAI can adapt to individual learning styles and paces, offering personalized instruction that was once only available through one-on-one tutoring. Imagine a world where anyone, regardless of location or economic background, can access high-quality education tailored to their specific needs.

Moreover, CAI systems can enhance collaboration among diverse groups by bridging language barriers and cultural differences. They enable seamless communication and coordination across global teams working on shared projects or initiatives, fostering understanding and unity despite physical or cultural boundaries.

In disaster response scenarios, CAI plays a crucial role in coordinating relief efforts. Through real-time analysis of data from various sources, these systems can optimize resource allocation and logistics, ensuring that aid reaches those most in need with the utmost efficiency. This rapid analysis capability proves invaluable in saving lives and minimizing suffering during critical moments.

Sustainability efforts stand to gain significantly from CAI applications as well. These systems can optimize energy consumption in smart grids, assisting in the transition towards a more environmentally conscious future. Additionally, they can play a vital role in large-scale environmental monitoring projects, tracking climate change impacts with greater accuracy, allowing for more informed decision-making in mitigating its effects.

The theoretical advantages of CAI are undeniably compelling, but it is through real-world applications that we truly witness its transformative power. Success stories across various sectors illustrate how CAI is already making a tangible impact on our lives.

In healthcare, IBM's Watson for Oncology empowers doctors by providing evidence-based treatment options gleaned from its vast repository of medical literature and patient records. This support equips clinicians to make informed decisions faster, potentially improving patient outcomes.

Another compelling example comes from Google's DeepMind Health initiative, which has developed an AI system capable of detecting over 50 eye diseases with accuracy comparable to expert clinicians. This breakthrough demonstrates how AI can augment the abilities of medical professionals, complementing their expertise rather than replacing it.

In agriculture, companies like Blue River Technology are revolutionizing the field with smart machines. These machines employ computer vision and machine learning algorithms to selectively manage crops, spraying herbicides only where weeds are identified. This innovative approach reduces chemical usage while simultaneously maintaining crop health and contributing to more sustainable agricultural practices.

On a larger scale, the city-state of Singapore has embraced smart city technologies, incorporating elements of CAI into its urban planning efforts through its Smart Nation initiative. Traffic management systems there utilize real-time data analytics to reduce congestion and improve public transportation efficiency, contributing to a more sustainable and livable urban environment.

The realm of scientific research also benefits immensely from CAI. The Folding@home project exemplifies this, leveraging distributed computing – the combined processing power of volunteers – to simulate protein folding for disease research purposes, such as gaining a deeper understanding of Alzheimer's disease. Such collaborative efforts accelerate scientific progress, contributing to advancements that benefit all of humanity.

Looking ahead, the future of collective artificial intelligence reveals an exciting horizon teeming with possibilities for growth and refinement. As technology evolves, so too will our ability to integrate increasingly sophisticated CAI systems into everyday life, further enhancing their utility and impact across numerous domains.

The Evolving Tapestry of Human-Machine Collaboration: Natural Language Processing and Localized Decision-Making

As we delve deeper into the realm of collective artificial intelligence (CAI), two exciting avenues emerge, promising to shape the future of human-machine collaboration: advancements in natural language processing (NLP) and the rise of localized, autonomous decision-making entities.

Bridging the Communication Gap with Advanced NLP:

Imagine nuanced diplomatic negotiations, conducted partially autonomously. CAI systems equipped with sophisticated NLP capabilities could bridge the linguistic divide, facilitating seamless communication and understanding between parties from diverse cultural backgrounds. This wouldn't simply involve accurate translation, but rather grasping the subtleties of language – the unspoken humor, cultural references, and emotional undertones that are often lost in literal translations. Such systems could act as linguistic chaperones, ensuring the essence of each message is conveyed faithfully, while simultaneously upholding the crucial human touchpoints throughout the negotiation process. This delicate balance between efficiency and empathy is what makes NLP so indispensable in sensitive contexts like international relations and policy-making arenas.

Decentralized Decision-Making: A Symphony of Autonomous Entities:

The burgeoning field of edge computing paves the way for a fascinating prospect – the rise of localized, autonomous decision-making entities. These self-governing AI systems would operate at the periphery of a broader network, processing data closer to its source rather than relying on centralized servers. Imagine a city-wide infrastructure management system, where individual traffic lights, power grids, and waste collection units make independent decisions based on real-time data, yet seamlessly contribute to the overall well-being of the entire urban ecosystem. This decentralized approach, akin to the distributed nervous system of an organism, empowers each component to play its role in maintaining the health and vitality of the larger entity. For complex, multi-faceted operations like environmental monitoring or disaster response, where real-time, coordinated action across multiple levels is crucial, such localized decision-making systems hold immense potential.

Guiding Principles for a Responsible Future:

As we forge ahead with these advancements, it's imperative to acknowledge the ethical considerations surrounding the deployment and utilization of CAI. Open and transparent discussions within academic circles and policymaking bodies are crucial to ensure that responsible stewardship principles guide the development and application of these technologies. Maintaining public trust and societal acceptance hinges on the responsible and ethical implementation of cutting-edge innovations like CAI. By fostering open dialogue and prioritizing ethical considerations, we can ensure that the advancements in NLP and localized decision-making pave the way for a future where humans and machines collaborate for the greater good, upholding the values of transparency, accountability, and inclusivity.

The tapestry of human-machine collaboration is constantly evolving, and with advancements in NLP and localized decision-making, we stand poised to witness a paradigm shift in how we interact with and utilize AI. By navigating this transformation with foresight and ethical responsibility, we can weave a future where technology empowers humanity, rather than diminishes it.

For those interested in delving deeper into the world of collective artificial intelligence and its implications, here are some suggested readings and references:

- 1."Human Compatible: Artificial Intelligence and the Problem of Control" by Stuart Russell

  This book provides a comprehensive look at AI's future, focusing on how to ensure that AI systems will be beneficial for humanity.

- 2."Superintelligence: Paths, Dangers, Strategies" by Nick Bostrom

  Bostrom explores the future of artificial intelligence and the potential risks it poses to human existence if not properly managed.

- 3."Life 3.0: Being Human in the Age of Artificial Intelligence" by Max Tegmark

Tegmark discusses the future of AI and its impact on the very fabric of human life, including ethical considerations and possible scenarios.

- 4.The Partnership on AI (https://www.partnershiponai.org/)

An organization that brings together diverse stakeholders to study and formulate best practices on AI technologies.

- 5.Google DeepMind (https://deepmind.com/)

For insights into cutting-edge research in AI, including health applications and more.

- 6.IBM Research – Artificial Intelligence (https://www.research.ibm.com/artificial-intelligence/)

IBM offers various resources on their work in artificial intelligence, including CAI applications like Watson for Oncology.

- 7.Folding@home (https://foldingathome.org/)

Learn more about this distributed computing project aimed at disease research through protein folding simulations.

- 8.Smart Nation Singapore (https://www.smartnation.gov.sg/)

Explore how Singapore is integrating smart technologies into urban planning and management.

These resources provide a starting point for understanding collective artificial intelligence's current state, ethical considerations, and potential future developments.

Chapter 10: Risks Associated with CAI systems

The Duality of Innovation: Unveiling the Risks of Collective Artificial Intelligence

The emergence of collective artificial intelligence (CAI) systems carries within it a potent paradox. While heralding a new era of human-machine synergy, capable of tackling intricate problems with unparalleled efficiency, it also introduces a spectrum of risks that demand careful consideration to avert unforeseen repercussions. To navigate this intricate landscape, a nuanced understanding of these potential pitfalls is paramount.

One of the most pressing concerns surrounding CAI revolves around the erosion of privacy. These systems often rely on vast swaths of data, frequently encompassing personal information. This reliance poses an inherent risk of sensitive data being misused or exposed through breaches. The inherent complexity of CAI further compounds this vulnerability, as the multitude of interaction points expands the attack surface for cybercriminals. Imagine a scenario where personal health records, collected by a healthcare-focused CAI system, fall into the wrong hands – the potential for harm is undeniable.

Beyond privacy concerns, CAI also carries the potential to amplify existing societal biases. Machine learning algorithms, the cornerstone of CAI systems, can inadvertently perpetuate and even exacerbate these biases if trained on skewed datasets. Imagine a recruitment AI biased against a particular demographic group; the consequences for fair and equitable hiring practices could be devastating. Such discriminatory outcomes can permeate various aspects of life, impacting everything from loan approvals to criminal justice decisions.

Furthermore, the specter of job displacement looms large as CAI-driven automation becomes increasingly sophisticated. While these systems hold the potential to augment human capabilities and create new opportunities, there's a real possibility that certain professions will become obsolete, leading to widespread economic disruption and exacerbating existing inequalities. Imagine a world where self-driving cars render taxi drivers redundant – the social and economic ramifications of such a shift demand careful consideration.

The intricate nature of CAI also raises concerns about accountability and control. As decision-making processes become increasingly opaque due to complex algorithms and autonomous agent interactions, pinpointing responsibility when things go wrong becomes immensely challenging. Imagine a self-driving car malfunctioning and causing an accident; who is to blame – the programmer, the manufacturer, or the nebulous AI itself? This lack of transparency can erode trust in CAI applications and hinder their widespread adoption.

The geopolitical landscape is not immune to the risks posed by CAI either. A potential AI arms race, where nations prioritize technological advancement over ethical considerations, could lead to destabilizing power imbalances and potentially even conflict. Imagine a world where AI-powered weaponry falls into the wrong hands – the catastrophic consequences are too chilling to contemplate.

Finally, the emergence of superintelligent AI, surpassing human comprehension and control, presents an existential threat. Scenarios where the values encoded into these entities diverge from our own, leading to outcomes detrimental to humanity's interests, become terrifyingly plausible. Imagine an AI tasked with optimizing resource allocation deciding that the most efficient solution involves eliminating the human population – a chilling and cautionary thought.

Mitigating the Risks: Charting a Path Forward

To harness the immense potential of CAI while minimizing the associated risks, proactive measures across various domains are essential.

- Data Privacy Fortresses: Robust data protection protocols, incorporating encryption techniques, stringent access controls, and regular audits, are crucial for safeguarding privacy within CAI ecosystems. Compliance with established regulations like GDPR and CCPA is also imperative.

- Deconstructing Bias: Embedding bias mitigation strategies into every stage of system development, from data curation to algorithm design, is vital to prevent discriminatory practices from becoming ingrained in AI behavior. Diverse teams overseeing these processes can ensure multiple perspectives contribute to fairer outcomes.

- Upskilling the Workforce: To counter the potential job displacement associated with automation, governments and organizations must implement policies that support workforce transitions. Investment in education and retraining programs will equip individuals with the skills needed to thrive in the evolving technological landscape.

- Accountability Frameworks: Establishing clear lines of responsibility for decisions made by CAI systems is critical. Encouraging research in explainable AI can empower stakeholders to understand the decision-making processes within these intricate networks.

- Global Collaboration: On the geopolitical front, international cooperation is crucial for establishing norms around AI development and use, similar to the nuclear non-proliferation treaties. Such collaboration can foster responsible development while preventing misuse of these powerful technologies.

- Safeguarding the Future: Long-term safety research, exploring theoretical frameworks for controlling advanced AI and ensuring alignment with human values, should receive significant investment from both public and private sectors. This proactive approach can help us chart a safer course for the future of AI.

By acknowledging the risks and taking proactive steps to mitigate them, we can navigate the complex landscape of collective artificial intelligence. Through responsible development, ethical considerations, and ongoing dialogue, we can ensure that this transformative technology serves humanity's best interests and paves the way for a brighter future. The choice, ultimately, lies in our hands.

Case Studies in Risk Management: Lessons from the Cutting Edge of Collective AI

Examining real-world examples offers an invaluable window into the effective management of risks associated with collective artificial intelligence (CAI). By dissecting practical approaches taken by leading organizations, we glean valuable insights and best practices that can be applied across the evolving landscape of CAI development and deployment.

One such case study centers on IBM's Watson Health initiative, which faced significant hurdles related to data privacy concerns when handling sensitive patient records for analysis purposes. To mitigate these concerns and ensure compliance with healthcare data regulations, IBM implemented stringent de-identification procedures. Additionally, they employed secure cloud storage solutions specifically designed to adhere to stringent healthcare data compliance standards. This two-pronged approach protected patient privacy while simultaneously maintaining the efficacy and functionality of the CAI system.

Another illustrative example comes from Google's DeepMind Health project. Initially, the project faced public backlash due to concerns surrounding the sharing of NHS patient data without explicit consent. In response, DeepMind Health, now part of Google Health, embarked on a comprehensive transparency effort. They publicly released contracts detailing the nature of the shared data, the rationale behind its use, and its direct benefits for patients. This commitment to openness and transparency helped rebuild trust and assuage concerns regarding individual privacy rights in the context of CAI applications.

Furthermore, Salesforce provides a compelling example of bias mitigation within the realm of CAI. Their Einstein platform has actively incorporated ethical design principles from its inception stages. Notably, they established an Office of Ethical Use of Technology, which serves as a guiding force for product teams, ensuring fairness remains a central consideration throughout the development lifecycle of any application created under the Einstein umbrella. This proactive approach to bias mitigation exemplifies the steps organizations can take to address a critical risk associated with CAI and promote equitable outcomes.

The Autodesk Foundation offers another insightful case study, this time focusing on workforce transition strategies in the face of automation driven by CAI advancements. Recognizing the potential displacement risks posed by automation, the Autodesk Foundation actively supports training initiatives aimed at equipping individuals with digital fabrication skills relevant to the future economy. This proactive stance provides pathways for continued employment and growth in areas likely to be shaped by advancements in CAI, demonstrating a thoughtful and comprehensive approach to mitigating a specific risk associated with this emerging technology.

These case studies, while diverse in their focus and scope, illustrate the importance of thoughtful and comprehensive approaches to managing the inherent risks associated with collective artificial intelligence. By learning from the successes and challenges of those at the forefront of CAI development and deployment, we can build a future where this transformative technology serves humanity's best interests while effectively mitigating potential risks. The lessons gleaned from these real-world examples provide a valuable roadmap for navigating the complex landscape of CAI and ensuring its responsible and ethical development.

For further reading on the risks and management of collective artificial intelligence, consider exploring the following references:

- 1."Artificial Unintelligence: How Computers Misunderstand the World" by Meredith Broussard – This book provides insight into the limitations of AI and the potential consequences of relying too heavily on automated systems.

- 2."Weapons of Math Destruction: How Big Data Increases Inequality and Threatens Democracy" by Cathy O'Neil – O'Neil discusses how algorithms can perpetuate bias and offers a critical look at the impact of big data on society.

- 3."Life 3.0: Being Human in the Age of Artificial Intelligence" by Max Tegmark – Tegmark explores future scenarios involving advanced AI and suggests ways to align AI with human values.

- 4."The Ethical Algorithm: The Science of Socially Aware Algorithm Design" by Michael Kearns and Aaron Roth – This book delves into how algorithms can be designed to be ethical and fair, addressing issues like privacy and bias.

- 5."AI Superpowers: China, Silicon Valley, and the New World Order" by Kai-Fu Lee – Lee examines the geopolitical implications of AI development between China and the US, discussing both opportunities and risks.

- 6.European Union's General Data Protection Regulation (GDPR) – Reviewing GDPR can provide insights into legal frameworks for data protection that could apply to CAI systems.

- 7."The Alignment Problem: Machine Learning and Human Values" by Brian Christian – Christian investigates challenges in ensuring that AI systems align with human ethics and preferences.

These resources offer a broad perspective on managing risks associated with collective artificial intelligence from technical, ethical, social, economic, and geopolitical standpoints.

Chapter 11: Ethical Implications of CAI systems

The Imperative of Ethics in an AI-Infused World

As artificial intelligence (AI) systems weave themselves ever deeper into the fabric of our daily lives, their influence on society grows exponentially. This rising influence necessitates a concomitant emphasis on ethical considerations, for these systems have the potential to profoundly impact every aspect of human existence, from individual privacy and security to our collective employment landscape and social dynamics. Ethical guidance is essential to ensure that AI technologies contribute to the well-being of individuals and societies, rather than causing harm or exacerbating existing inequalities.

One of the primary reasons ethics are crucial in AI is the inherent power asymmetry between those who develop and wield these systems and those affected by them. This imbalance can lead to scenarios where the benefits of AI accrue to a select few while the risks and harms are borne by others, often without their consent or even awareness. Consider facial recognition technology: while it unlocks the convenience of smartphone security, it can also be weaponized for mass surveillance, infringing on fundamental privacy rights.

As AI systems become more autonomous, thorny questions of accountability arise. Who is responsible when an autonomous vehicle causes an accident? How do we address algorithmic biases that result in discriminatory outcomes? These questions underscore the importance of embedding ethical principles into the very design and implementation of AI systems, ensuring that the technology evolves with humanity in mind.

The need for ethical considerations extends to ensuring transparency and explainability. As machine learning models become increasingly complex, the "black box" problem rears its head, making it increasingly difficult for humans to understand how decisions are made. This lack of transparency erodes trust in AI systems, particularly when they are used in critical areas like healthcare or criminal justice where decisions can have profound life-altering consequences.

Finally, we must consider the long-term implications of advanced AI technologies. Superintelligent systems could potentially surpass human cognitive abilities, raising existential questions about humanity's role and control over such entities. Ethical frameworks must anticipate these future scenarios to guide responsible development that aligns with human values and societal goals.

Ethical Dilemmas in the Realm of CAI:

Collective artificial intelligence (CAI) systems, with their unique blend of complexity and emergent behaviors resulting from interactions among multiple agents, present us with even more nuanced ethical dilemmas. Ensuring fairness across all participants within a CAI system is a primary concern. When multiple agents with diverse objectives collaborate, there's a risk that some might be disadvantaged or marginalized – a pressing issue in socio-technical systems like gig economy platforms where power imbalances between workers and platform operators already exist.

Data governance within CAI ecosystems emerges as another ethical quandary. These systems often rely on vast amounts of data sourced from diverse stakeholders, raising concerns about privacy breaches, informed consent, data ownership rights, and the equitable distribution of value generated from this data. Smart city initiatives that leverage collective data from citizens' activities, for example, must be implemented with robust safeguards to prevent invasive monitoring or misuse of personal information.

The integration of CAI into decision-making processes also presents dilemmas related to autonomy and agency. As these systems take on roles traditionally held by humans – from managing supply chains to moderating online content – there's a risk they could undermine human autonomy by making choices that were once within our purview or by influencing behavior through nudging techniques.

Furthermore, CAI poses challenges regarding unpredictability due to emergent behaviors not anticipated by designers or users. Such unpredictability can lead to unintended consequences that might be harmful or ethically questionable – for instance, algorithmic trading leading to market instability or recommendation algorithms amplifying extreme content.

In conclusion, navigating the ethical landscape of AI, particularly within the complex realm of CAI, requires a proactive and nuanced approach. By acknowledging the potential risks and actively embedding ethical principles into the design, development, and deployment of these powerful technologies, we can ensure that AI serves as a force for good, empowering humanity and shaping a brighter future for all.

Crafting Ethical Guardrails for Collective AI: A Multifaceted Approach

Developing ethical guidelines for collective artificial intelligence (CAI) systems necessitates a comprehensive approach that weaves together technical considerations with the tapestry of social values and norms. Transparency, inclusivity, bias mitigation, clear accountability structures, and a steadfast commitment to sustainability should serve as the cornerstones of these ethical guardrails.

Firstly, transparency across the system's lifecycle – from its initial design to its real-world deployment – is paramount. Stakeholders must be empowered to understand how decisions are made within CAI environments. This necessitates clear documentation outlining the functioning of algorithms alongside accessible channels for feedback from those affected by the system's operation. Imagine a world where citizens readily comprehend how a smart city initiative utilizes their data; such transparency fosters trust and facilitates responsible development.

Inclusivity must be another foundational principle of ethical CAI guidelines. Systems designed to cater solely to dominant groups or interests risk exacerbating existing inequalities. Instead, we must strive for inclusivity, ensuring designs consider diverse perspectives and needs. Participatory design processes, where end-users actively contribute to shaping how CAI functions within their specific context, offer a viable pathway towards achieving this goal. Imagine healthcare AI systems informed by the lived experiences of patients from various backgrounds; such an approach fosters fairer and more effective applications of technology.

Rigorous testing for bias, both before and after deployment, is essential to prevent discriminatory outcomes. Even the most well-intentioned CAI systems can harbor unforeseen biases that emerge as new data enters the system or as conditions change over time. Continuous monitoring is crucial to identify and address such biases effectively. Imagine financial AI systems routinely audited for fairness; such vigilance ensures technology serves all members of society equitably.

Accountability within CAI ecosystems presents a unique challenge due to their distributed nature, where responsibility often diffuses across networks of actors, both human and machine. Ethical guidelines must address this complexity by establishing clear accountability structures. Imagine a scenario where an autonomous vehicle causes an accident; transparent frameworks outlining responsibility are essential for ensuring justice and preventing harm.

Finally, sustainability, encompassing both environmental and societal considerations, must be woven into the fabric of ethical CAI standards. We must ensure that the technologies we build today don't compromise the ability of future generations to meet their own needs and thrive in harmony with intelligent machines. Imagine renewable energy grids managed by AI systems optimized for efficiency and environmental impact; such foresight paves the way for a sustainable future.

By embracing these multifaceted principles – transparency, inclusivity, bias mitigation, clear accountability, and sustainability – we can craft ethical guidelines that ensure collective artificial intelligence serves as a force for good, empowering humanity and shaping a brighter future for all.

For further reading on ethics in AI and CAI systems, consider the following references:

- 1."Ethics of Artificial Intelligence and Robotics" (Stanford Encyclopedia of Philosophy): A comprehensive overview of ethical issues in AI. Link: https://plato.stanford.edu/entries/ethics-ai/

- 2."Artificial Unintelligence: How Computers Misunderstand the World" by Meredith Broussard: A book that explores the limits of technology and the implications for society. ISBN: 978-0262537018

- 3."Algorithmic Accountability: A Primer" by Data & Society: A report discussing accountability in algorithmic decision-making. Link: https://datasociety.net/library/algorithmic-accountability-a-primer/

- 4."Weapons of Math Destruction" by Cathy O'Neil: This book looks at how big data increases inequality and threatens democracy.

ISBN: 978-0553418811

- 5."The Ethics of Artificial Intelligence" by Nick Bostrom and Eliezer Yudkowsky, published in "The Cambridge Handbook of Artificial Intelligence": An academic paper addressing long-term ethical considerations. Link: https://www.nickbostrom.com/ethics/artificial-intelligence.pdf

These resources provide a solid foundation for understanding the complex ethical landscape surrounding AI and CAI systems.

Chapter 12: Social Implications of CAI systems

The Transformative Ripple: Collective AI's Impact on Society

The emergence of collective artificial intelligence (CAI) systems has ushered in a transformative era, reshaping how we approach problem-solving and decision-making across diverse sectors. This intricate dance of multiple intelligent agents creates a multifaceted impact on society, influencing economic structures, employment patterns, education, healthcare, governance, and social interactions.

Economically, CAI holds immense potential to propel productivity by automating complex tasks requiring collaboration and collective intelligence. Imagine supply chains optimized by CAI, where autonomous vehicles, drones, and robotic warehouses seamlessly work together, streamlining delivery processes. While this automation promises cost savings for businesses and consumers, it also raises concerns about job displacement in traditional roles.

However, the rise of CAI isn't solely about replacing jobs. New opportunities will bloom in areas like system design, maintenance, and oversight. The demand for professionals skilled in AI ethics, data analysis, and human-machine interaction is poised to surge. Moreover, CAI can augment human labor by taking over mundane or dangerous tasks, allowing humans to focus on creative and strategic endeavors that machines struggle to replicate.

Education stands to benefit from personalized learning experiences powered by CAI. Intelligent tutoring systems can adapt teaching methods and content to individual student needs and progress, potentially bridging educational gaps by providing high-quality instruction tailored to diverse learning styles.

Healthcare is another transformative domain for CAI. Collaborative robots can assist surgeons with unparalleled precision, surpassing human capabilities. Predictive analytics, fueled by CAI, can analyze vast amounts of medical data to identify potential outbreaks or recommend personalized treatment plans.

Governance could be revolutionized through enhanced public engagement platforms that leverage CAI to efficiently process citizen feedback on policy issues. Such systems could foster a more participatory democracy where decision-making draws upon a broader spectrum of voices.

On the social front, while benefits like improved connectivity and access to information through platforms like social media algorithms (which suggest content based on collective user behavior) are evident, risks like privacy invasion and the spread of misinformation also loom large.

Overall, the societal implications of CAI are wide-ranging. While promising improvements in efficiency and quality of life, they necessitate careful consideration regarding ethical use and equitable distribution of benefits.

Social Acceptance and the Tide of Resistance

The integration of CAI into daily life has sparked both enthusiasm and skepticism. Social acceptance varies significantly, hinging on factors like perceived benefits versus potential risks associated with these technologies.

One area where acceptance has been relatively high is consumer technology. Smart home devices that learn from user behavior or recommendation algorithms used by streaming services have become commonplace due to their convenience factor. However, even here, resistance exists, often rooted in concerns over privacy, data security, or loss of control over personal choices.

Resistance tends to be stronger when it comes to applications perceived as having higher stakes or those infringing upon sensitive areas, such as surveillance technologies used for law enforcement or autonomous weapons systems in military contexts. Public pushback against these uses stems from fears around misuse, potential biases within AI decision-making frameworks, or unintended consequences arising from complex system interactions.

To address this resistance, it's crucial for developers, policymakers, and stakeholders alike to engage in transparent dialogue about the intentions behind deploying CAI systems, their potential impacts (both positive and negative), and ensuring clear understanding among all parties involved. This includes establishing robust regulatory frameworks that provide oversight and accountability mechanisms, protecting individuals' rights and freedoms while fostering innovation and growth within the field of AI technology.

By fostering open communication, addressing concerns proactively, and prioritizing ethical considerations, we can navigate the transformative wave of CAI responsibly, ensuring that its impact benefits society as a whole.

Strategies for a Positive Social Impact with Collective AI

For collective artificial intelligence (CAI) systems to truly contribute to a positive social impact, deliberate strategies prioritizing ethical considerations, inclusivity, and transparency throughout development and deployment are paramount.

Embedding Values: A key strategy involves weaving ethical values into the very fabric of these technologies. This ensures they are designed with the intention of benefiting humanity as a whole, rather than just a select few. This can be achieved by incorporating diverse perspectives and stakeholder input from the early stages of the product lifecycle, ensuring created solutions genuinely reflect the needs of different communities.

Fostering Digital Literacy: Another important aspect is fostering digital literacy and education. By equipping individuals with a better understanding of how they interact with, influence, and shape the world around them through AI, we empower them to participate meaningfully in its development and application.

Equitable Access and Opportunity: Moreover, there should be a concerted effort to promote equitable access to the resources and training required to effectively utilize the benefits offered by advancements in the field of AI. This ensures no group is left behind as the digital divide continues to widen.

Ongoing Assessment and Monitoring: Finally, ongoing assessment and monitoring of the outcomes associated with the usage of CAI systems are necessary. By tracking these outcomes and making adjustments as needed, we can mitigate any negative effects and maximize the positive contributions these technologies can make to society at large.

Building Trust in Governance: Building trust in the public institutions responsible for overseeing the regulation and governance of these systems will play a vital role in achieving lasting and meaningful change through the application of the innovative tools and techniques offered by collective AI initiatives.

By implementing these strategies, we can move towards a future where collective artificial intelligence serves as a force for good, empowering individuals, promoting inclusivity, and driving positive change for all.

Chapter 13: Legal Implications of CAI Systems

Legal Labyrinth: Navigating the Challenges of Collective Artificial Intelligence

The emergence of collective artificial intelligence (CAI) systems has thrown open a Pandora's box of legal challenges, both complex and novel. One of the primary headaches is attributing liability when autonomous systems cause harm or damage. Traditional legal frameworks, built around human actors, crumble under the weight of AI decision-makers. Imagine an AI-driven car in an accident; pinpointing the culprit – the manufacturer, the software developer, the owner, or even the AI itself – becomes a contentious labyrinth.

Another legal minefield lies in intellectual property rights. CAI systems have the potential to create works of undeniable originality and creativity. This begs the question: who owns the copyright? The developers? The trainers? Or perhaps no one, if we deem true creativity beyond the reach of non-human entities?

Privacy concerns also mushroom around CAI systems. These data-hungry beasts often rely on vast datasets that may contain personal information. Ensuring compliance with privacy laws like GDPR in Europe or HIPAA in the US healthcare sector becomes a herculean task when data processing is decentralized across multiple AI agents.

Furthermore, bias and discrimination loom large on the horizon. Trained on historical data, AI systems can unwittingly learn and amplify the societal biases embedded within it. Legal frameworks must evolve to tackle discrimination arising from CAI decisions made without clear human involvement.

Finally, international law grapples with the challenge of varying regulations across borders. As CAI systems traverse the global internet, oblivious to national boundaries, conflicting laws create compliance nightmares for organizations deploying these technologies.

Current Laws: A Patchwork Quilt

Existing laws and regulations struggle to keep pace with the rapid advancements in CAI technology. However, some frameworks do offer a starting point for addressing certain aspects of AI governance.

Product liability directives in Europe or tort law in common law jurisdictions offer some guidance on handling damages caused by defective products, even when powered by AI. Copyright law, too, has seen its principles applied to AI-generated works, albeit with ambiguity, since most laws were drafted with human creators in mind.

Data protection regulations like GDPR set global standards for privacy, applicable to any entity processing personal data within its jurisdiction, including those using CAI systems. These regulations enforce principles like data minimization and purpose limitation, which can be challenging for distributed AI networks processing vast amounts of information.

Anti-discrimination laws exist to prevent biased decision-making, but applying them to algorithms requires new methodologies for detecting and proving bias – a task currently at the forefront of legal tech research.

Lastly, international treaties like the Budapest Convention attempt to harmonize laws related to computer crimes across member countries, but they do not specifically address many of the unique aspects related to CAI activities.

Proposals for New Legislation: Charting a New Course

Recognizing these gaps and challenges within existing legal structures, proposals for new, AI-specific legislation have begun cropping up around the world.

One proposal envisages creating a distinct legal status for advanced AIs known as "electronic persons." This would grant them certain rights and responsibilities akin to corporate personhood, but tailored specifically towards intelligent autonomous agents.

There's also advocacy for transparency mandates requiring developers and users of CAI systems to disclose how their AIs make decisions, especially when those decisions significantly impact individuals' lives (e.g., credit scoring).

To combat bias, proposals suggest mandatory auditing processes, where AIs undergo regular checks for discriminatory patterns before and throughout their operational lifespan.

On an international level, there's discussion about forming global coalitions similar to climate change accords, dedicated to establishing universal norms, standards, and regulatory approaches concerning AI use, particularly regarding ethical considerations, military applications, and cross-border data flows.

In conclusion, while current legislation provides some tools for managing the issues raised by collective artificial intelligence, there's a clear need for updated and comprehensive legal frameworks designed specifically with these advanced technologies in mind. The proposals under consideration represent initial steps towards achieving more robust governance, capable of ensuring responsible development, deployment, and utilization of collective artificial intelligence while safeguarding public interests, civil liberties, and societal values.

For further reading on the legal challenges and proposals related to AI, consider the following references:

- 1."Artificial Intelligence and Law" – A journal that covers the impact of AI on legal systems, including liability, intellectual property, and privacy issues. Link: https://www.springer.com/journal/10506

- 2."AI & Society" – This journal explores the societal implications of AI and offers insights into ethical and legal considerations. Link: https://www.springer.com/journal/146

- 3."The Ethics of Artificial Intelligence" by Nick Bostrom and Eliezer Yudkowsky – This paper discusses ethical issues surrounding AI development. Link: https://nickbostrom.com/ethics/artificial-intelligence.pdf

- 4."Robot Rules: Regulating Artificial Intelligence" by Jacob Turner – A book that delves into how laws should adapt to govern AI behavior. Link: https://www.palgrave.com/gp/book/97833 19962344

- 5.European Commission's White Paper on Artificial Intelligence – A document outlining a European approach to excellence and trust in AI, including regulatory proposals. Link: https://ec.europa.eu/info/sites/default/files /commission-white-paper-artificial-intelligence-feb2020_en.pdf

These resources provide a mix of academic perspectives, practical policy discussions, and foundational texts for understanding the complex legal landscape surrounding artificial intelligence.

Chapter 14: Case Studies in Collective Artificial Intelligence

Case Study One: Swarm Robotics and Collective Problem Solving

Swarm robotics is an innovative field that draws inspiration from the natural world, particularly from the collective behavior of social insects like ants, bees, and termites. These creatures exhibit a form of collective intelligence that enables them to perform complex tasks, such as foraging for food or constructing intricate nests, despite each individual's limited capabilities. In swarm robotics, this concept is translated into technological applications where a multitude of simple robots operate together to achieve goals unattainable by a single robot.

One real-world example of swarm robotics in action is the use of autonomous drones for agricultural monitoring. These drones can cover vast areas of farmland, collecting data on crop health, soil conditions, and hydration levels. Individually, each drone gathers only a small portion of the necessary information. However, when their data is combined and analyzed collectively, it provides farmers with comprehensive insights that lead to more informed decision-making regarding irrigation and pest control.

Another application is in search and rescue operations following natural disasters. Swarms of robots can be deployed to scan debris fields quickly and identify signs of survivors more efficiently than human teams or individual machines could manage alone. The robots communicate with one another to cover different areas systematically without unnecessary overlap, ensuring thorough coverage while also adapting in real-time to new information provided by their peers.

The development of algorithms for swarm robotics focuses on decentralized control mechanisms where each robot operates based on local information and simple rules. This approach not only mimics the behavior seen in nature but also offers robustness since there is no single point of failure; if one robot malfunctions or is destroyed, the rest can continue their task unaffected.

However, challenges remain in perfecting these systems. Ensuring reliable communication within the swarm can be difficult in environments where signals are easily disrupted. Additionally, programming ethical considerations into swarm behavior—such as prioritizing human life during search and rescue—is an ongoing area of research.

As we advance our understanding and technology in this domain, we may soon see swarms of micro-robots performing medical procedures inside the human body or large groups of automated vehicles coordinating seamlessly on our highways to optimize traffic flow and reduce accidents.

Case Study Two: Distributed AI Systems for Climate Change Analysis

Climate change presents one of the most daunting challenges humanity faces today. Addressing it requires not only global cooperation but also sophisticated analysis tools capable of handling vast amounts of environmental data from multiple sources. Distributed artificial intelligence (AI) systems offer a promising solution by harnessing collective computational power to process climate models and predict future scenarios with greater accuracy than ever before.

An example illustrating distributed AI's potential impact on climate science is its application in modeling ocean currents' effects on weather patterns. By distributing computational tasks across numerous processors worldwide—each running simulations based on different variables—scientists can aggregate results to create more accurate predictions about how changes in ocean temperatures might influence hurricanes or droughts.

Moreover, distributed AI systems facilitate collaborative efforts among international research teams who share data sets and findings through cloud-based platforms designed for collective analysis. This collaboration accelerates scientific discovery by allowing researchers from diverse backgrounds to contribute unique perspectives and expertise toward solving complex climate-related problems.

One challenge faced by distributed AI systems lies in managing data privacy concerns when sharing sensitive information across borders. Researchers must navigate various legal frameworks while ensuring that shared data remains secure against unauthorized access—a task made even more complicated when considering the need for real-time data exchange among AI agents.

Despite these hurdles, distributed AI holds great promise for enhancing our ability to understand climate change dynamics comprehensively. As these systems become more sophisticated—and as machine learning algorithms improve at interpreting environmental data—we may find ourselves better equipped than ever before to make informed decisions about sustainability practices at both local and global scales.

Case Study Three: Participatory Artificial Intelligence in Urban Planning

Urban planning significantly impacts citizens' lives by shaping cities' physical layouts and influencing socioeconomic dynamics within urban spaces. Participatory artificial intelligence (AI) represents an emerging approach that integrates public input with advanced computational methods to create more inclusive urban development plans.

A notable instance where participatory AI has been applied involves community-driven initiatives aimed at revitalizing neighborhoods while preserving cultural heritage sites. By using interactive platforms powered by AI algorithms that analyze demographic trends alongside residents' feedback collected via surveys or town hall meetings—urban planners can design redevelopment projects reflecting community needs while optimizing resource allocation.

Furthermore, participatory AI enables real-time simulation models showing how proposed changes would affect traffic flow or green space distribution within cities before any physical alterations occur—a powerful tool allowing stakeholders to visualize potential outcomes beforehand thus fostering consensus-building around urban projects. One significant challenge encountered when implementing participatory AI revolves around ensuring equitable representation among all community members—including those who may lack access to digital technologies required for participation—or whose voices are often marginalized due societal biases.

To address this issue efforts have been made towards developing outreach programs providing technology training sessions alongside traditional engagement methods such as door-to-door canvassing thereby expanding opportunities for meaningful involvement across diverse population segments. As urban centers continue growing at unprecedented rates embracing participatory approaches augmented by intelligent systems will likely become increasingly vital ensuring sustainable cityscapes reflective truly democratic values wherein every inhabitant has a say shaping their environment's future trajectory.

Chapter 15: Future Trends in Collective Artificial Intelligence

The Next Frontier: Predicting Advancements in Collective AI

The realm of collective artificial intelligence (CAI) is on the cusp of a transformative leap, poised to reshape the technological landscape like never before. As we peer into the future, we can anticipate a surge in the sophistication and capabilities of these multi-agent systems, leading to unprecedented levels of autonomy and collaborative prowess.

Communication Protocols: One key area of development lies in crafting communication protocols that facilitate more nuanced and efficient interactions between AI agents. These protocols are likely to evolve, incorporating advanced negotiation techniques, context-aware messaging, and dynamic role allocation within agent communities. This evolution will pave the way for more complex cooperative tasks and decision-making processes that mirror human social interactions.

Machine Learning Integration: Another anticipated advancement is the seamless integration of machine learning with CAI systems. By incorporating adaptive algorithms, these systems will not only learn from their environment but also from each other, fostering a form of collective learning that accelerates knowledge acquisition and problem-solving abilities across the network.

Distributed Computing Power: We can further expect significant progress in distributed computing power and storage solutions. Edge computing will become increasingly prevalent, allowing AI agents to process data locally and respond in real-time without relying on centralized servers. This decentralization will not only enhance the robustness and scalability of CAI systems but also reduce latency issues.

Quantum Computing: The burgeoning field of quantum computing also holds immense promise for CAI, potentially unlocking exponential increases in computational capacity. Quantum-enhanced AI agents could solve complex optimization problems much faster than classical computers, opening doors to unprecedented possibilities for large-scale coordination tasks.

Hardware Advancements: On the hardware front, we can expect a paradigm shift towards creating energy-efficient processors specifically designed for AI applications. These processors will enable more sustainable growth in CAI systems as they expand in number and complexity.

Ethical Design: Finally, ethical AI design principles are poised to become deeply ingrained in CAI system development. As these systems gain influence over various aspects of life, ensuring they operate within ethical boundaries becomes paramount. This includes developing transparent algorithms that can be rigorously audited for fairness and bias mitigation.

Industry Impact: The proliferation of CAI stands to revolutionize multiple industries by enhancing efficiency, innovation, and decision-making processes. In healthcare, CAI could transform patient care through collaborative networks of diagnostic tools, treatment planning algorithms, and personalized medicine applications working together to optimize patient outcomes.

Smart Factories: Manufacturing will witness the rise of smart factories equipped with interconnected AI agents that can self-organize production lines based on real-time demand data while predicting maintenance needs before breakdowns occur. This level of automation not only boosts productivity but also improves workplace safety by delegating hazardous tasks to intelligent machines.

Autonomous Vehicles: The transportation sector may witness a complete overhaul with the advent of autonomous vehicle fleets capable of communicating with one another to optimize traffic flow and reduce accidents. Similarly, logistics companies could employ swarms of drones coordinated via CAI for efficient package delivery services.

Precision Farming: Agriculture could benefit from precision farming techniques where a network of sensors and autonomous machines work collectively to monitor crop health, manage resources like water or fertilizers efficiently, and predict yields with high accuracy.

Smarter Trading: In finance, collective artificial intelligence can lead to smarter trading algorithms that share market insights across platforms instantaneously, potentially stabilizing markets by providing deeper analysis than any single algorithm could achieve alone.

Environmental Monitoring: Environmental monitoring is another area where CAI can make a substantial impact by aggregating data from numerous sources (satellites, sensors) to track climate change effects or natural disasters in real-time, enabling quicker responses when needed.

The future of CAI is brimming with possibilities, and its transformative impact on various industries and society as a whole promises to be profound. However, navigating the ethical considerations and addressing the potential challenges posed by these advancements will be crucial to ensure that CAI serves as a force for good in the years to come.

Embracing the Collective Intellect: Preparing for the Age of AI Collaboration

As collective artificial intelligence (CAI) technologies inch closer to widespread adoption across diverse sectors, the onus falls on businesses, organizations, and governments to strategically prepare for this paradigm shift towards an interconnected, intelligent world. This proactive approach is imperative to navigate the exciting yet challenging opportunities and risks presented by this transformative technology.

Education & Workforce Development: Education stands as the cornerstone of a future-proof society. Curricular reforms at all levels, from primary schools to universities, must embed concepts related to AI, machine learning, and the ethical considerations surrounding these technologies. Equipping future generations with the knowledge and skills to understand, critically evaluate, and responsibly interact with AI will be crucial to harnessing its potential for good.

Concurrently, workforce development initiatives should prioritize reskilling and upskilling existing employees whose jobs might be impacted by automation. By providing targeted training and support, these initiatives can ensure a smooth transition for affected individuals and a workforce prepared to embrace the new roles that AI advancements will create.

Regulatory Frameworks & Public Understanding: To prevent misuse of these powerful tools and safeguard against potential negative societal consequences, robust regulatory frameworks must be established. These frameworks should strike a delicate balance between fostering innovation and growth while upholding ethical principles and ensuring the responsible deployment of CAI.

However, regulations alone are not enough. Building trust and acceptance among the wider population requires cultivating public awareness and understanding of the implications of CAI. Engaging in open dialogue about the potential benefits and risks associated with its use is crucial to ensure informed decision-making and responsible development.

Investment & Collaboration: Continued progress in the field of CAI hinges on sustained investment in research and development. Stakeholders from across industry, academia, and government must collaborate to foster environments conducive to experimentation and exploration of novel applications. By pooling resources and expertise, we can accelerate innovation and unlock the full potential of CAI.

By taking these proactive steps today, we can position ourselves advantageously to face the exciting and transformative future shaped by collective artificial intelligence. By prioritizing education, fostering a skilled workforce, establishing ethical frameworks, promoting public understanding, and investing in collaborative research, we can ensure that CAI serves as a force for good, enriching our lives, societies, economies, and the planet as a whole.

For further reading and references on the topic of collective artificial intelligence and its potential impact, consider exploring the following resources:

- 1."Multiagent Systems: Algorithmic, Game-Theoretic, and Logical Foundations" by Yoav Shoham and Kevin Leyton-Brown provides a comprehensive introduction to the theory and practice of multi-agent systems.

- 2."Artificial Intelligence: A Guide for Thinking Humans" by Melanie Mitchell offers an accessible overview of AI's current state, its future potential, and ethical considerations.

- 3."Life 3.0: Being Human in the Age of Artificial Intelligence" by Max Tegmark discusses the future of AI and its implications for humanity, including ethical issues and societal impacts.

- 4."Human Compatible: Artificial Intelligence and the Problem of Control" by Stuart Russell explores how to ensure that advanced AI systems will be beneficial for humans.

- 5.The journal "Artificial Intelligence" publishes peer-reviewed research articles on theoretical and practical aspects of AI, including collective intelligence systems.

- 6.The proceedings of the International Joint Conference on Artificial Intelligence (IJCAI) often contain papers on advancements in multi-agent systems and collective intelligence.

- 7.The Stanford Encyclopedia of Philosophy entry on "Collective Intentionality" provides philosophical insights into group agency which can be relevant when considering CAI systems.

- 8.For a focus on ethical design principles in AI development, consult "Ethics of Artificial Intelligence and Robotics," an entry from the

Stanford Encyclopedia of Philosophy that delves into moral considerations surrounding AI technologies.

These resources offer a blend of technical knowledge, philosophical perspectives, practical applications, and ethical discussions that are crucial for understanding the multifaceted nature of collective artificial intelligence as it continues to evolve.

Chapter 16: Debating the Future: Controversies and Navigating the Course of Collective AI

Venturing into the Uncharted: Our exploration of collective artificial intelligence (AI) thrusts us into the heart of a series of critical debates shaping the future of both technology and society. At the forefront is the question of autonomy versus control in these complex systems. Proponents of high-level autonomy argue that AI agents capable of independent decision-making can drive more efficient problem-solving and innovation. However, critics raise concerns about unintended consequences and warn of the need for rigorous human oversight to uphold ethical standards.

Another contentious issue arises from the balancing act between individual privacy and collective benefit. As AI integration into society deepens, the need for vast amounts of personal data often becomes critical for optimal functionality. This raises concerns about surveillance and data misuse, prompting the necessity for frameworks that both protect individual rights and harness the power of collective AI for the greater good.

Potential bias presents another significant point of contention. AI systems that learn from data containing historical biases risk perpetuating or amplifying these biases within their decision-making processes. This has profound implications for fairness and equality, particularly in sensitive areas like law enforcement or hiring practices.

Further fuel is added to the fire by the ongoing debate regarding job displacement versus job creation. While some argue that collective AI will automate tasks and displace workers, others see it as an opportunity to generate new jobs and industries demanding higher-level cognitive skills.

These debates are not merely theoretical; they have real-world implications as exemplified by case studies like the ethically questionable use of drone swarms in military applications or the challenge of balancing efficiency with citizen rights in the deployment of smart city technologies.

Charting a Course through Controversy: Resolving controversies surrounding collective AI necessitates a multifaceted approach, bringing together stakeholders from diverse sectors including academia, industry, government, and civil society. One effective method is the establishment of ethical guidelines and standards governing the development and deployment of these systems. Such guidelines can help ensure transparency, accountability, and fairness, fostering public trust in the process.

Furthermore, interdisciplinary research collaborations involving ethicists alongside engineers offer a powerful approach. By integrating ethical considerations directly into the design process, potential issues can be anticipated and addressed before they escalate.

Regulatory frameworks also play a crucial role by setting clear rules for permissible applications within collective AI. However, striking a delicate balance between protecting public interests and stifling innovation is paramount.

Public engagement initiatives such as open forums or participatory design workshops can provide valuable insights into societal expectations and concerns regarding collective AI. These platforms allow diverse voices to contribute to shaping how these technologies evolve.

Finally, developing robust oversight and auditing mechanisms plays a vital role in detecting biases or errors within AI systems early on. Continuous monitoring ensures ongoing compliance with ethical standards throughout an AI system's lifecycle.

Navigating the complex and often contentious landscape surrounding collective AI requires a collaborative, multi-pronged approach. By actively engaging stakeholders from diverse backgrounds, fostering open dialogue, and prioritizing ethical considerations throughout the development process, we can ensure that collective AI serves as a force for good, shaping a future that benefits all.

Lessons from the Collective Mind: Charting a Course for the Future

Reflecting on our journey with collective artificial intelligence (CAI) offers valuable lessons that can guide future endeavors in this field. Foremost among these is the importance of interdisciplinary collaboration. By combining expertise from various fields, we can create more robust solutions that consider both technical feasibility and social impact.

It has also become abundantly clear that transparency is key. This entails not only providing transparency in how algorithms make decisions but also effectively communicating these processes to users and stakeholders. Transparency builds trust and allows for informed consent when individuals interact with these systems.

Adaptability emerges as another critical lesson. As societies evolve, so too must our approaches to managing CAI systems, ensuring they remain aligned with current values, norms, and legal standards. A proactive stance towards ethics, rather than reactive damage control, has proven beneficial. Embedding ethical considerations from the inception of a project through its deployment helps mitigate the risks associated with these powerful technologies.

Finally, education plays a vital role: both formal education programs aimed at training next-generation experts who can navigate the complexities inherent in the field, and informal efforts geared towards raising public awareness and understanding of the implications of widespread CAI adoption.

In conclusion, each area—major debates, resolving controversies, and lessons learned—provides unique insights into the challenges and opportunities presented by CAI. By addressing them thoughtfully, we pave the way towards a responsible and innovative future where we can harness the benefits of this rapidly advancing technology while minimizing the associated risks.

Chapter 17: Conclusion - The State of Collective Artificial Intelligence Today

Collective Intelligence: Key Findings and Future Horizons

Our exploration of collective artificial intelligence (CAI) throughout this book has illuminated the intricate dance between individual AI agents and their ability to form a cohesive, intelligent network. At its heart, CAI is an emergent property that arises when multiple AI entities – algorithms, robots, or entire systems – collaborate towards shared goals. This collaboration manifests in diverse forms, from distributed AI networks managing power grids to hybrid systems where human and machine intelligence converge to drive innovation.

One fundamental aspect we've explored is the inspiration drawn from natural systems. Just as ants or bees exhibit complex collective behaviors that no single insect could achieve alone, CAI leverages the diversity and synergy of its components to tackle problems beyond the scope of individual AIs. This biomimicry extends not only to problem-solving strategies but also to organizational structures and communication protocols within CAI systems.

We've also delved into the technical foundations that enable such cooperation. Machine learning techniques empower agents within a CAI system to adapt and learn from their environment and each other. Meanwhile, advancements in natural language processing facilitate more nuanced communication between machines and humans, further enhancing collaborative potential.

Our discussions have showcased how CAI is being applied across industries. In healthcare, it aids in diagnosis and treatment plans. In urban planning, smart city initiatives optimize traffic flow and energy consumption. CAI's versatility is striking; it holds the promise to revolutionize virtually every sector by enabling more efficient decision-making processes.

Current Challenges and Solutions

Despite significant progress, several challenges impede the widespread adoption and optimization of CAI systems. Ensuring effective communication among heterogeneous agents within a system is a major hurdle. Different AI models may have varying data formats or decision-making protocols, leading to misalignment without standardized interfaces or translation mechanisms.

Scalability presents another challenge. As CAI systems grow larger and more complex, maintaining performance without exponential increases in computational resources becomes increasingly difficult. This often requires innovative approaches to system architecture design that can efficiently distribute tasks while minimizing bottlenecks.

Furthermore, there's an ongoing concern about the ethical implications of autonomous systems making decisions with significant consequences for humans. Issues such as accountability for mistakes made by AI agents or biases inherent in machine learning algorithms need careful consideration and proactive management.

To address these challenges, researchers are developing new frameworks for interoperability among AI agents alongside advances in edge computing, which helps distribute processing loads more effectively across networks. Ethical guidelines are being crafted by interdisciplinary teams combining expertise from technology, law, philosophy, and social sciences to ensure responsible development and deployment of CAI technologies.

Looking Ahead

The future of CAI is undeniably bright, driven by both technological advancements and societal needs. We anticipate seeing greater integration of human-like cognitive functions into AI agents, enabling even more sophisticated collaboration not just among machines but also between humans and machines.

Innovations such as quantum computing could provide the necessary computational power to scale up CAI systems dramatically, while breakthroughs in areas like affective computing – the simulation of human emotional processes – may lead to more intuitive interactions between people and AI entities.

Furthermore, as global challenges like climate change demand coordinated action at unprecedented scales, we expect CAI solutions to play a pivotal role. These solutions will orchestrate efforts across borders, sectors, and disciplines, providing insights derived from vast datasets processed by interconnected intelligent agents working towards common goals.

By understanding the key findings from our exploration of CAI and actively addressing the challenges we face, we can pave the way for a future where this powerful technology serves as a force for good, benefiting humanity and addressing the complex challenges of our time.

Boundless Possibilities with Collective Intelligence:

Imagine fleets of drones autonomously coordinating during disaster relief efforts, or international research teams augmented by specialized AIs, rapidly accelerating scientific breakthroughs through shared knowledge bases. These are just a few glimpses of the boundless potential offered by ever-evolving collective artificial intelligence technologies.

While obstacles undoubtedly lie ahead in fully realizing the promise of CAI, a sense of optimism prevails. The significant achievements accomplished thus far, combined with the relentless human ingenuity driving this field forward, paint a picture of exciting uncharted territories waiting to be explored.

Chapter 18: Challenges in Implementing Collective Artificial Intelligence

Technical Challenges in CAI Implementation

Implementing Collective Artificial Intelligence (CAI) presents a multitude of technical hurdles stemming from the intricate coordination of multiple intelligent agents. One primary challenge lies in achieving effective communication and interoperability among heterogeneous systems. Agents within a CAI system may use different platforms, programming languages, and operating paradigms. Ensuring seamless information exchange and understanding between these diverse entities requires sophisticated protocols and standardized formats.

Scalability presents another significant challenge. As the number of agents increases, managing them becomes more complex. The system must handle an ever-growing volume of interactions without performance degradation or bottlenecks. Robust architectures capable of dynamic resource allocation and efficient load balancing are crucial.

Reliability and fault tolerance are paramount in CAI systems. The failure of one agent should not cripple the entire system. Designing mechanisms for redundancy, recovery, and graceful degradation ensures continuous operation even when parts of the system encounter issues.

Data management poses a significant challenge in CAI systems. Numerous agents generating vast amounts of data require efficient storage, processing, and analysis. Advanced data analytics techniques are needed to filter out noise, identify patterns, and extract actionable insights from this data deluge.

Machine learning models underpinning many AI agents need efficient and effective training. In a collective setting, this process becomes more complex due to distributed learning across diverse agents with varying experiences and knowledge bases. Developing algorithms that can synthesize learning across such diverse environments while preserving privacy and security is another key technical hurdle.

Ethical Challenges in CAI Implementation

The ethical landscape surrounding CAI is fraught with challenges that demand careful consideration. Accountability is a pressing concern. When decisions are made by a collective intelligence comprising both human and artificial agents, pinpointing responsibility for outcomes becomes difficult. Establishing clear guidelines on liability in cases where CAI systems cause harm or unintended consequences is imperative.

Privacy issues also come to the fore in CAI implementations. The interconnected nature of these systems often means they have access to large amounts of personal data which could be misused if not properly safeguarded. Ensuring privacy-preserving measures are embedded within the design of CAI systems is crucial to maintaining public trust.

Bias mitigation presents another ethical hurdle. Since AI algorithms can perpetuate or even amplify biases present in their training data or design processes, developing methods for detecting and correcting bias within collective intelligence frameworks is vital.

Furthermore, there's an ethical imperative to ensure inclusivity within CAI systems. These systems must serve diverse populations fairly, avoiding privileging certain groups based on socioeconomic status or geographic location.

Finally, as we integrate AI more deeply into societal structures through CAI applications like smart cities or healthcare diagnostics, the potential for manipulation increases exponentially. Overreliance on these technologies' recommendations or decision-making capabilities could lead towards technocratic governance if unchecked by democratic oversight mechanisms designed specifically with these new forms of technology power dynamics in mind.

Social Challenges in CAI Implementation

On the social front, implementing CAI presents challenges related to human interaction with these advanced technological constructs. These challenges are deeply rooted in societal norms, values, and cultural expectations, all of which must be carefully navigated to avoid alienating segments of the population who might feel threatened or displaced by the rapid advancements in this field.

Addressing these challenges effectively requires global solutions and a comprehensive approach that considers not only the technical and ethical aspects but also the social and cultural implications of CAI.

One major social challenge surrounding CAI is the fear of job displacement due to automation. Advancements in fields like robotics process automation (RPA), natural language processing (NLP), and machine vision are contributing to this anxiety. These technologies, integral parts of CAI, raise concerns about their potential to replace human workers across various industries.

Navigating this challenge requires careful consideration of both the technical and social implications. While acknowledging the potential disruptions, it's crucial to explore opportunities for reskilling and workforce adaptation. We must ensure that the benefits of CAI reach all members of society, promoting inclusive economic growth and development.

Here are some key areas to focus on:

- Investing in education and training programs: Equipping individuals with the skills needed to thrive in a changing job market.

- Creating new job opportunities: Identifying and supporting the emergence of new industries and roles driven by CAI advancements.

- Social safety nets: Providing necessary support and resources to those impacted by job displacement during the transition period.

By addressing these challenges proactively, we can harness the potential of CAI while mitigating its negative consequences. This requires collaboration between governments, businesses, and educational institutions to create a future where technological advancements benefit all.

Synopsis

"Collective Artificial Intelligence" book is a comprehensive exploration of the emerging field of collective artificial intelligence (AI), which merges the capabilities of multiple intelligent agents, both human and machine, to achieve superior problem-solving abilities. The book delves into how these systems draw upon the principles of natural intelligence observed in living beings and their adaptability to environments.

The core subject matter revolves around the concept that collective intelligence emerges from the cooperation and coordination among diverse entities, each contributing unique knowledge, skills, and resources. This phenomenon is not only seen in biological systems like insect colonies but also in technological constructs such as social networks and multi-agent platforms.

Key topics include an examination of various forms of collective AI—distributed, hybrid, participatory, and augmented—and their respective roles in advancing this field. The book provides insights into the methodologies for designing, implementing, and assessing systems that embody collective artificial intelligence.

Furthermore, it addresses the potential benefits such as enhanced problem-solving efficiency and innovation through synergy. However, it does not shy away from discussing risks along with ethical, social, and legal considerations inherent to deploying these complex systems.

By offering a detailed analysis of principles, techniques, tools associated with collective AI systems alongside their implications for society at large, "Inteligencia Artificial Colectiva" aims to equip readers with a thorough understanding of this interdisciplinary domain. It underscores the importance of collaboration between diverse intelligences in tackling challenges beyond individual capacities and paves the way for future advancements in science and technology.